Rucksack to Briefcase

A civilian-side, job-hunting guide for service members & their families!

Chief Warrant Officer Raymond

Rucksack to Briefcase: a civilian side job-hunting guide for service members and their families
© 2014 Chief Warrant Officer Raymond

Edited, cover designed and prepared for publication by
The PassionProfit™ Company

Published by The DR Company
The DR Company
P.O. Box 19214
Sugar Land, TX 77496-9214
info@civilianside.com
(832) 301-5110

All rights reserved. This book may not be reproduced in whole or in part, or transmitted in any form, without written permission from the author and publisher, except by a reviewer who may quote brief passages in review.

Retail Cost: $14.95
ISBN-10: 1494963701
ISBN-13: 978-1494963705

Printed in the United States of America

TABLE OF CONTENTS

Dedication
Acknowledgements & Coach Credit
Introduction: For Friends and Family of Service Members
Chapter 1: A Mile in Your Boots 7
Chapter 2: The Art of Transition 29
Chapter 3: The Art of Communication 37
Chapter 4: Your Resumé 45
Chapter 5: Job Hunting 65
Chapter 6: A Vital Q&A 77
Chapter 7: Alfred: A Case Study 87
Chapter 8: The Interview 93
Chapter 9: Michelle: A Case Study 105
Chapter 10: Beyond Employment 109
Bonus: A Master Checklist 115
A Final Word From Chief Raymond 116
     Appendix 117
  What the Military Will Never Tell You 118
  Chief Raymond's Deployment Survey 122
  A Resumé Improvement Workshop 127
  Sample Resumés for Federal Job 137
  Online Resources for Service Members 154
  Glossary of Military Terms 158
  About Chief Warrant Officer Raymond 161

DEDICATION

This book is dedicated to the men and women who *have* served, *currently* serve, and who *will* one day serve selflessly in the active duty or reserve components of the Army, Navy, Air Force, Marines, Coast Guard, as well as the Army and Air National Guards.

DISCLAIMER

The views and opinions expressed in this book are those of the author and do not necessarily reflect the official policy or position of any agency of the U.S. government.

ACKNOWLEDGEMENTS

I first wish to thank God for blessing me with the seed of knowledge, wisdom and understanding as well as the skills and ability to share my experience. I thank God for surrounding me with people who have poured into me and encouraged me to bring forth a relevant message in the form of a book.

I wish to thank my wife, Trenice, for her unyielding support during the completion of this project. I want to thank her for her unconditional love, and to let her know I could not have completed this book without her standing by my side. I am thankful for my beautiful children, Taquana, Ariel, Elaine and Christina and my grandson Jalen. All of you are my source of joy and give me the reason and the courage to stay the course and set the example.

I am eternally grateful to all the individuals who've crossed my path and the positive as well as negative experiences they have contributed to my personal and professional development.

Coach Credit

I would also like to give credit to my coach, mentor, editor, and most of all my friend, Walt F.J. Goodridge. I am thankful for his longtime friendship and most of all his business knowledge, coaching expertise, vision, motivation and editing to help me see the project through to completion. He kept me focused and in the game when things got tough and distractions were present. Thanks, Walt, for holding me to task at different phases of the project.

Walt is a well-documented professional and he held me to a high standard as he does all his clients. (www.passionprofit.com)

For Friends & Family of Service Members

Even if you've never been a military service member, it is possible you are the friend or relative of someone who has completed, or is returning from military duty. Military service is a very unique experience. When an individual is deployed overseas, relationship bonds develop, worldviews change, and the service member often returns an entirely different person after having lived an entirely different reality. It is for this reason that the process of transitioning *back* into civilian life—what I refer to as "civilian-side or home deployment"—is such a challenge. Success requires the understanding and cooperation of the service member as well as friends and family. It is rarely a one-person affair.

In our society, much of an individual's self-esteem, sense of accomplishment, value and identity hinges on the ability to care for those he or she loves. Towards that end, therefore, this book focuses on one aspect of civilian-side transition: finding employment. It offers some insights into the challenges our service members face, tips on resumé-writing, strategies for job-hunting, advice on interviewing, a few case studies, plus a little motivation.

While it was written to speak directly to the service member, this book can also help you, the friend, relative, hiring agent, co-worker and even future employer, to gain some insight into some of the unique challenges civilian-side transition entails. (There's even a glossary in the Appendix to help you learn a little "military-speak.") Thank you for taking the time to read it!

--**Chief Warrant Officer Raymond**

*A warrant officer is the subject matter technical expert in his/her field. The commissioned officer, as visionary, plans strategy. The enlisted non commissioned officer handles operations to fulfill the goals of the officer in charge, while the warrant officer consults both the officer and non-commissioned officer in the process of how things will get done.

Chapter 1
A Mile in Your Boots

"I realize that 99% of the population has not served in the military. However, I think most support your service and sacrifice. I believe, for the most part, those who have not served simply do not fully understand what you do, day in and day out whether you are deployed or stationed state side. I do not know if most understand fully the sacrifices you make." —**Leon Panetta, former Defense Secretary**

First Things First

You can call me Chief Raymond. However, what's more important than who *I* am, is who *you* are, and I mean that sincerely.

You are a member of a small group of less than 1% of the entire population who has served or is serving in the US armed forces. If you have seen combat, or have been deployed to a combat area, you are part of an even smaller group of men and women who have borne the cost of war, sacrificed, risked and given lives on the battlefield. As stated in the quote above by the 23rd former Defense Secretary, Leon Panetta, most people do not understand the sacrifices you have made.

I do.

I begin this book, therefore, by saluting you, the fine men and women of the US military and the service you've provided, and you, likewise, can render and return the custom and courtesy honor of a hand salute.

Yes, I know the sacrifices you've made, and I also know the unique challenges of transitioning back into the civilian sector after such an experience and after years of service. You may have hundreds of convoys under your belt, been in several fire fights, and survived other life-threatening situations that people working in civilian-side business will simply never understand. And even though what you have seen, experienced and contributed to your country is rare and vitally important in the overall scheme of things, its *value* simply does not translate or convert well to the world of civilian business. Therein lies the fundamental challenge of going from rucksack to briefcase.

Your military service and experience simply have no civilian-side equivalent that can demonstrate to a private business owner how his bottom line will be affected or how an investor will receive a positive "return on investment" for what you have done. Similarly, a businessperson who has experience generating millions of dollars in revenue for a company will not seem to be of great help to you in a firefight. Each of you brings equally important skills to the table.

Now, imagine you and a potential employer are sitting across from each other at such a table—a job negotiation table—observing and discussing a coffee cup. This metaphoric cup is filled with the experiences and qualifications you've each brought to the table. Depending on where you are sitting, and how the cup is positioned, the reality of that cup will appear slightly differently to each of you. The handle, for instance, may be visible to one person and not the other. The actual contents of the cup may be visible or not. The writing on the side of the cup, too, may be obscured, etc. The bottom line, however, is that it's still a cup of qualifications that have value. The immediate visibility of the handle does not make that cup more or less important to either party. Once they can succeed in communicating the value of the cup to each other, both parties can use the value within that cup to accomplish their individual agendas.

My goal for you by the end of this book is that you be able to find and "get a handle" on *your* cup, and be able to speak clearly about it in a language that is understood by the civilian sector, so that others get a handle on it as well, and clearly understand the cup of qualifications and value you bring to the table and that you can offer to their team or organization.

Who am I?

Like many of you reading this book, I am a war veteran. I deployed twice and served with our sister branches, the Navy, Marines and Air Force, as well as in our reserve components.

I am also a certified human resources professional with over ten years recruiting experience, and 4½ years as an Army "foot recruiter" in the New York City Recruiting Battalion where I received numerous awards for recruiting excellence. The remainder of my experience has been in the civilian sector, which, I believe, qualifies me to offer guidance on this subject.

I am a well-seasoned military recruiter in the oil and gas industry, and served as a personnel recruiter for an international offshore drilling company reviewing thousands of resumés, conducting interviews, doing telephone screenings and hiring candidates to fill job positions around the world. Because of my military background, I am the "subject matter expert" on all things military and who handles calls and correspondence from veterans.

I understand very well the adjustment process one goes through when transitioning from the military back to the civilian sector because I have done it. I understand what you have done, what you *continue* to do and how valuable your contributions are because I've walked more than a mile in your boots down the same path, and I wanted to offer a simple, practical, step-by-step manual to help you and others through that process.

If you grasp what I am going to share with you in this book, it will put you on a good pace toward transitioning smoothly back into the civilian sector and landing great employment. This is true and applicable for E-1s to E-9s, W1s to CW5s, O-1s to O-10s, family members, and even any DOD (Department of Defense) employees in light of the sequestration and furloughs taking place.

It is doable. It is achievable. Most of all, *you* can do it!

Personally, and for the record, as a veteran who knows what you've been through, I believe there *should* be a veterans' preference for civilian-side hiring, and special provisions for your time of service if that service entailed some level of disability or severe injury—especially if the job you are seeking is within a government agency.

However, as you prepare to transition, do not—I repeat: *do not*—proceed with an expectation that the civilian sector owes you anything. Instead, put the expectation on *yourself* that you will be prepared and competitive for the market place and positions you seek. Market yourself so that you are in demand and can *earn* the position not because of any entitlement, but because you are best qualified for the position. Yes, sometimes in the real world, the best person is not always selected—decisions may be based on who you know—but, that is just how it is sometimes. So you have to get yourself mentally prepared to compete and work hard to make yourself competitive when applying for and landing that post-military job. Yes, life is all about change and dealing with the unexpected. You can do it! You are an expert in dealing with change as you dealt with it the entire time you served at home and overseas in combat or non-combat environments. With that said, let me share my own rucksack to briefcase story.

My Story, and How it Can Help You

As a veteran returning from a tour in Iraq, I was faced with the sobering reality of transitioning back into the civilian work force. Like many, I learned it can be challenging whether you've served six months, two years, or an entire career in the military.

I found it challenging because, quite simply, there was not a single, simple guide by someone who knew what it was like to be a service member that offered the tools necessary to make it a smooth transition given our unique reality. My fellow service members and I went through ACAP (Army Career and Alumni Program), FFSC (Fleet and Family Support Center) training, and the TAP (Transition Assistance Program) classes during which we received books and tips to make the transition happen for us. These "how to" guides did provide clear actions that needed to be taken as well as simple and concise tools to be successful. However, the ACAP briefing, for instance, was offered no less than 90 days prior to leaving the service. In other words, we had to take it *while* we were actually still "on mission." Therefore, the challenge was figuring out how to balance the obligations of your unit's mission while at the same time focusing on trying to have a smooth transition more than 90 days later. TAP, on the other hand, simply didn't provide enough time to thoroughly prepare for a smooth transition. However, these two courses were all the preparation we had, and so, we received them with the military's best intentions.

Rucksack to Rejection

With two deployments under my belt, a successful military career, and the ACAP and TAP trainings, I thought, at the time, it would have been an easy road to obtaining employment. However, things did not go as smoothly as I had imagined. No callbacks. No interviews. I struggled during this period trying to figure out what I was doing wrong. What did I need to do to increase my chances of being successful? I asked anyone I felt could help me. First, I was told I needed a better resumé, so I went to a professional company to help me write one. The company requested my military information and created a four-page resumé that listed everything I ever did in the military. It was a great looking resumé...for another military deployment, that is! The resumé was not shaped in such a way to highlight my relevant *civilian-side* skills. Any company looking at that resumé would not understand what I brought to the table or how their bottom line could be improved by having me as a part of their team. It had too much information and was way too long. The results: still no callbacks; still no interviews. I was successfully going from rucksack to rejection!

Here's what I learned from that experience: resumé companies are good at plugging information into a software program and, with the click of a button, they can produce a resumé you *think* will have companies knocking down your door to hire you. Things didn't quite work out that way. One reason for this, I discovered, is that the people creating these resumés—more often than not—do NOT have any military experience at all! Or even if they do, they aren't well informed about translating that military experience into what companies are really looking for.

Rucksack to Resumé, and...

Finally, after months of struggle and frustration, I was fortunate enough to run into some people—true professionals—who helped me improve my skills, tighten up my resumé and they pointed me in the right direction. The first step, once again, was getting a better resumé, but this time, based on what they taught me, and my discipline in implementing it, I started receiving calls and getting interviews, until I finally landed my first job! I had done it! I had gone from rucksack to (better) resumé, then from resumé to briefcase!

Going from rucksack to briefcase was, for me, a long four-month process that stirred up the passion in me to start giving back to others who may not have been as fortunate as I was. I vowed to help others—especially my brothers and sisters in the armed forces. I knew there had to be a simpler way for our service members, or anyone else for that matter, to better prepare for and succeed in their transition and obtaining employment in the civilian sector.

How my story can help you

Earlier, I mentioned some of the challenges with ACAP (Army Career and Alumni Program) and TAP (Transition Assistance Program). These programs offer some ideas on how to approach civilian-side transition. However, they do not prepare you well enough for what to expect in real transition engagement. In my opinion, the classes should also provide mock interviews. (I do not recall going through mock interviews when I transitioned, but since then, I believe the courses have been upgraded, and service members now do get to practice.)

The fleet and family support centers also offered classes as well, but with so many people transitioning and retiring, these classes cannot provide the individual attention required.

Since these programs all take place during service, a service member also has to get the unit and leadership to approve the necessary time off in order to take the class or training—potentially compromising that service member's responsibilities within the organization.

The bottom line is that after completing anywhere from two to twenty years of service, getting three days or a week of transition training these programs provide is simply not enough to get a service member fully prepared to transition successfully into meaningful employment. Think about it: the military gives you *six months to a year* of training to prepare to go to war, but *less than a week* to get ready transition back to civilian employment. While it's true that civilian life is "the norm," people don't realize that a certain amount of transition preparation is necessary to ease back into civilian life. They don't realize how much a person or a society can change when that person is away in military service.

Therefore, based on my transition experience, here are 10 suggestions to help you achieve a successful rucksack to briefcase transition for yourself:

1. Start your transition plan *immediately*! (i.e. the day you *decide* to retire or transition!)

2. Transition is full-contact engagement. Be proactive and on offense in preparation.

3. Take responsibility for your success and get the training you need.

4. Start networking early through some of the social media forums I'll share with you later.

5. Seek out local resources for help in resumé writing and mock interviews.

6. Look for work even *while* you have a job with the military. (tip: use your leave time)

7. Do not wait until the last minute to start applying for these jobs.

8. Seek intern and part-time opportunities where you can get paid and gain experience at the same time.

9. Interview as frequently as you are able in order to generate the maximum number of offers.

10. The military is a business. Do not expect to get time off to prepare or train for transition.

Additional Transition Resources available in the appendix and online at civilian-side.com

10 Ways Military Experience has made you UNFIT for a job

Has military service made me UNFIT for a job? Being in the military is a unique experience that may actually make you *unfit* for traditional employment. (Note: When someone in an active component of the military returns from deployment, their job is still the military. Therefore, this question is more for the reservist who returns from deployment to resume civilian-side life.) Here are some of the realities of life after the military that tens of thousands experience every day.

1. *Substance Abuse.* Among many service members, there is often an increase in the use of alcohol and drugs to help distract from and dilute the emotional effects of the tragedies of war they have experienced. I know service members who've lost their jobs and families or who find themselves in drug rehabilitation programs after their battlefield experience.

2. *Lack of current civilian-side work experience.* After completing my first deployment, and faced with release from active duty, I had no idea what I was going to do as career. This was the first time I had even heard about resumés and cover letters or interviewing for a job. I, like many others, found myself behind the curve.

3. *Not being understood/no commonality.* Many service members fear that people at a civilian job will simply not be able to relate or understand them given their unique military experience. They fear that the camaraderie and trust they enjoyed in the military will not exist civilian-side.

4. *Anxiety.* The uncertainty of the job market and the uncertainty of finding a job with the equivalent pay and benefits the military offered can lead to anxiety. For reservists on multiple deployments, there is the anxiety of whether their job will be there when they return. *Will the company still be in business? Will I be laid off? Will I be in the same position when I return?*

5. *Self-doubt.* I can tell you from my own experience that with transition came doubts about my self-worth. I simply did not believe I could be considered valuable to an organization with civilian-side goals and objectives. *Will they take into consideration my service abroad and sacrifice to the country? Will my military background be seen as an asset or liability?*

6. *Lack of motivation.* At times during my transition, I felt unmotivated, isolated and helpless. It felt so much easier to do my old job in the military than it did to go online, fill out job applications and go through the long, drawn out submission and interview process.

7. *Guilt.* At other times, service members feel unworthy and guilty about getting a well-paying civilian-side job with good benefits while some of the people they deployed with are struggling, or simply did not even make it back home. *Why me and not them?*

8. *Lack of structure.* Some people thrive best within structure and regimentation. Although they have the freedom to do what they wish civilian-side, many service members do not believe a civilian position will have the rigid structure, the regulations, conformity, the ordered community and predictability the military offers.

9. *Alienation.* Some service members feel, as a result of their military experience, civilians, who have never experienced military reality, may treat them as an outsider.

10. *Isolation/separation.* For an infinite number of reasons, service members sometimes feel the need to simply get away, to isolate and separate themselves from family, friends and community. Such feelings can wreak havoc on a civilian-side career.

The bottom line of all of the above reasons is *fear* of some kind or another. For some of us, our time in the military involved living 24 hours a day in life and death situations. Sometimes, you can bring that fear back with you, and thereafter perceive and respond to everything and every detail of everyday life as having life or death consequences.

The new civilian-side environment does, in fact, present a unique set of threats that require adjustment. *Can I, or will I adjust to the new norm in this new environment?* That is the basic fear many service members bring with them to civilian-side transition.

12 Ways the Military *Prepares* You for Employment

On the other side of the coin is the question: *"Could the fact of my military service actually help me in my search for employment?"* To answer that question, here's feedback from service members around the world:

"By being in the military...."

1. *"I learned the importance of timeliness."* If you are on time to meetings, you are probably late. The standard in the military was to be at least ten minutes *early*. Everything in the military, especially operations, is based on the synchronization of time. Every element and component depends upon another, and an entire operation can fail if each element is not executed in a timely matter.

2. *"I pay more attention to detail."* While on deployment, you learn to notice small differences in the layout of the street, subtle differences in the population, people's moods and facial expressions, etc. These little details can offer clues to the operations of combative forces. In the military, the little details can save your life.

3. *"I am more safety conscious."* In the military, you learn how to stay safe. You conduct risk assessment to identify the potential risk of an operation, as well as how to mitigate that risk. That skill is equally valuable on the civilian side, where the protection of life and equipment means increased profits to a civilian business.

4. *"I work until the job is done."* When you are deployed on a military mission, you can't clock out after 12, 18 or even 24 hours. You continue the mission until it is complete or until you are properly relieved.

5. *"I manage and use resources more efficiently."* In the military, you might find yourself on a mission with limited resources necessary for the mission as well as your safety and survival. You learn how to manage those resources and use them efficiently.

6. *"I perform regular maintenance."* In the military, maintenance is conducted on equipment, as well as on yourself to insure that both you and your equipment are ready when the orders are given.

7. *"I can work effectively in teams."* In the military, you learn teamwork from day one. You are typically assigned to a unit or organization based on your job training and skill level—not based on whom you know. Consequently, you get to work with a diverse, often multi-cultural team.

8. *"I am better at public speaking."* Researchers have discovered that the average person's greatest fear is that of public speaking. At some time in your military career, you *will* find yourself standing in front of a small or large group making announcements, giving instructions or teaching a course to your peers.

9. *"I have a more global perspective."* Living in different countries, learning new languages, interacting with people with different worldviews is all part of overseas deployment. Such experience and the awareness it provides can be invaluable while civilian-side, too.

10. *"I work well under pressure."* In the military, it is a given that you be able to work under pressure and adjust under fire.

11. *"I am a better planner."* In the military, when you are assigned a mission, you are also given the mission's intent/desired end result. Therefore, everyone from leadership to the individual service member has to "backward plan" from the end result to his/her individual tasks in order to accomplish the mission.

12. *"I am an avid goal setter."* In the military, you learn how to set goals and are held to a certain standard of excellence. You are also held accountable for your actions or lack thereof.
[See Appendix for responses from individual service members]

How the military has helped you

To successfully transition from rucksack to briefcase, your task—like the men and women quoted above—will be to discover *your* new military-honed skillset and identify what you bring to the table as a result of your military training. How does that skillset match the job you are seeking? When I applied for my civilian-side job as a recruiter, I did not have industry-specific experience. However, military training had developed my ability to identify people's strengths and match them to the right job. With that basic ability in place, I knew that the actual specifics related to the industry would simply require a bit of learning. I was able to take stock of my military strengths and demonstrate to my employer that I was the one for the job. That is what you have to do. No one else knows you better than you know yourself. You will be the one who has to demonstrate to the employer that you have the skills to fix their problem. With that said, here are a few that you learned during your service—whether you realize it or not:

Analytical skill: In the military, when your unit is given a mission, you are either a leader or subordinate. You analyze the intent of the mission. You determine what role your organization plays in the overall scheme of things. You determine the role *you* play as an individual in the scheme of things. You have to set timelines starting with the end in mind. Analytical skill is now part of your arsenal of abilities.

Project management: As the leader in the military, you performed the following tasks:
1. conduct mission decision making process (MDMP)
2. determine necessary equipment, inspect and assure equipment as well as personnel readiness.
3. inspect the team or section
4. conduct rehearsals
5. execute the mission
6. conduct an "after action review" to determine what happened, what was supposed to happen, what things were done well, and what needs improvement. That is called "project management."

Strategic Analysis, Planning and Execution: Everything you do in the service involves some strategy. The strategy to get from objective A to objective B includes anticipating all the possible challenges you may face (rough terrain, bad weather, hostile forces, etc.), and formulating contingency plans to accomplish the mission. In the military, mission failure is not an option. This skill and "failure is not an option" mindset are extremely valuable and transferrable to corporate objectives. Companies need strategists when the market is bad, when sales are down, when there is a natural disaster, etc., and in many cases, their success will determine the life or death of the company.

Teamwork: **Teamwork** is critical and has been instilled in you from your first day in basic training. It starts with a team of two or more battle buddies who fit within a larger group who fit within a larger group all the way to the commander in chief. You are taught to be, and are held accountable for your as well as your buddy's actions. You are taught to look after your buddy and him/her to look after you. Even our elite service members, who may work individually at some portion of a mission, still have teams they are a part of.

Realize this: You served in the most diverse, multicultural international organization in the world whether you led a team or were a teammate. You served in joint service cross-functional environments, where if you are Army serving with Navy, or Marines with Air Force you needed to quickly understand not only the language but the different dialect as well. You served with coalition forces as a part of an international team that required language, dialect as well as cultural sensitivity and training.

This unique skill set is of tremendous value and highly transferable to any local, national and international civilian company. When given the opportunity, your mission is to effectively communicate to the potential employer or hiring official your ability to work with diverse teams. *I served on diverse project teams to accomplish goals.... I demonstrated teamwork while serving as an_____ during deployment to_____."* This is your opportunity to hit it out of the park during an interview! Demonstrate how this attribute will add to the overall success of the department/company you are about to join. You have collaborated, planned contributed to the success of teams. Remember you can do more and are more productive with a top producing team.

Discipline and focus under pressure: Discipline is a critical skill that kept you safe and alive during your local service and worldwide deployment. You learned the importance of discipline during basic training and it is something that is now ingrained in you. Something as simple as exercising "noise, light and litter discipline" can have life and death consequences.

Remaining focused under the pressure is second nature to you. You may have been part of a convoy and if that convoy comes under attack, you have to remain focused and make split-second decisions that may mean life or death for you or your teammates.

This is an important transferable skill that companies are looking for and you my brethren in arms possess that skill. You have the discipline to arrive early and stay late until the mission is complete. You can perform and produce and will remain focused in harsh environments and under pressure and when plans go awry.

Mission-Orientation: This is another area in which service members excel. I dare say you will likely give a civilian-side worker a run for the money in this category. In the military, once assigned a task, your goal is the accomplishment of the mission; not sticking to the standard nine-to-five work schedule. While deployed, you worked 16-20 hour/7 day workweeks for the duration of your deployment! (Little do the civilian-side hiring officials know that *their* 40-hour workweek feels to you like you're getting your hours cut!)

Think about how critical and transferable this mission oriented skill is. How well would things have gone if, when you were stationed on a submarine on a mission, or out of the wire on a convoy as a Marine or Soldier, or flying on a refueling mission with the Air Force, you were focused on what your hours of work were? Not well at all. That's why you and I are taught to be committed to the mission and its accomplishment. This is the kind of commitment companies are looking for, but they will not know you bring this attribute to the table unless you tell them.

And don't be afraid to tell them! Tell them about the time you were deployed on a short submarine mission and were informed you were being extended in order to support the efforts of your sister unit. Or tell them that while out on convoy you were heading back to base camp when you received a radio call that another convoy was in the vicinity and needed supplies and some additional support. Your day was over but the mission was not and you did what was necessary to contribute to mission success.

Training skills: Your ability to receive, process, adopt and implement various types of training is an important and transferable ability. You are trained at entry level (basic training), advanced training for your specific job, leadership, cross training, and specialized formal training. The part of our background that has more weight civilian-side is the cross training you received. In the military you received receive training on new equipment, safety regulations, and specialized abilities regardless of your primary job. This "cross discipline" training is highly attractive to a civilian company.

High Production: High productivity is what you learned in basic training and improved as you advanced through your military career. You know how to push yourself beyond your limit. You know how to extract just a bit more water from the stone; go the extra mile! From physical fitness exams—more push-ups=more points—to getting assets to fellow service members locally and globally, you know that to become the best fighting force in the world, you have to out-produce your competition.

That military-ingrained habit of high productivity has stayed with me in everything I do. During my tenure as a foot recruiter in the Army in the streets of New York and Westchester county, there was an inner drive to be recognized as the top producing recruiter in the organization as well as nationwide.

High production equates to high returns. When you produce, you affect the bottom line of the organization even for a non-profit organization as the military. Make sure you have a few examples of your high productivity to communicate to the hiring official during your interview.

Accountability and Responsibility: These are two of the most critical attributes and skills that you will transfer to a civilian company. Even those of us in the military fail to recognize or realize that the equipment we are trained to operate often costs millions, even billions of dollars. You will be accountable for sensitive items such as weapons, multi-million dollar aircraft and billion dollar warships. You are responsible for the maintenance, safe operation and the whereabouts of the equipment assigned to you. If something happens to your equipment you are held accountable and responsible.

You are also accountability for human resources—the 5 to 10, 40 to 120, or 5,000 brave men and women on your team. This is a tremendous responsibility.

Gather examples of the things you were assigned and to include their dollar value. Describe the number as well as the geographic placement of the people you were responsible for. Companies are looking for these skill sets and you need to be able to communicate your level of responsibility effectively to your potential new employer.

Human Resource and Management skills: In the military, human resources (people) management was your bread and butter, and no one does it better than you. Human Resource Management includes managing retention, support and development of your staff through mentoring, employee relations and supervision. In the military, you have trained people to get them up to standard and promoted, you have insured that soldiers were trained and ready to deploy worldwide at the direction of the commander in chief. As a human resources planner, you assessed the knowledge and competency of your staff and trained, developed or rotated them as necessary. You made sure your staff were paid according to rank and years of service. You developed your staff through counseling and performance reviews.

Whether you're a squad leader, a platoon sergeant, a division commander or combat engineer, you accomplish mission objectives through the management of people.

As ex-military, your management skills are impeccable whether you are the project manager or part of the management team. Be sure you communicate this basic military skill to the hiring official during your interview.

The Bottom Line: The truth is, you have gained a tremendous amount of experience and maturity as a result of your military training. These traits, habits and perspectives the military has honed in you can make you a more valuable employer, manager and ultimately CEO in the civilian sector. Your task and challenge in going from rucksack to briefcase is simply to get a better at understanding of this and speaking to what the prospective employer or business owner needs or wants.

Chapter Summary: The Harsh Reality

The reason there are not many more official veteran employment resources is that, quite simply, while the nation would love to treat you special for your years of service, the harsh reality is that once you return civilian-side, you're pretty much on your own on the same playing field as everyone else.

Transitioning from the military to the civilian sector is challenging for everyone who experiences it. Furthermore, while your service history does not guarantee employment, and while some of your military experience may have left you unfit for employment in some ways, the truth is that if you start planning early, and realize that in other ways, your military experience has made you the ultimate civilian-side employee or CEO, and become good at communicating that fact, you can and will achieve a successful rucksack to briefcase experience!

***

One of the things I hope you grasp by reading this book is this very important point. You have to temporarily set aside your competitive spirit and that internal drive to be successful *on your own*. The fact is, you are making a transition from a very familiar culture to one that you are bit removed from since you entered the service. Embrace a spirit of humility and try this approach: practice saying the words: *"I need your help."* I know that may be challenging because you are not used to asking for help. You have led large organizations of soldiers to battle, taught hundreds of sailors in training, mentored senior and junior airman, officers and marines in the most complex of technological advanced missions. You are used to hearing *"make it happen, sailor, marine, soldier, figure it out!"*

However, here on the civilian-side, people are rooting for you and want you to succeed, but no one will know you need assistance unless you ask for help. Forget the rank that is upon your chest or collar, be flexible and ask the professionals for assistance and feedback, guidance and direction. Try it. It works. It's not a sign of weakness.

Now, not everyone will have the time or the interest to help, but if you let it be known and keep asking, knocking, seeking and letting people know, then eventually you'll find the ones who do. The second part of my advice is that really apply the information you receive. It is not one size fit all. Refine it and customize it until you become confident and proficient and until you land the ultimate transitional job.

So be receptive, reflective, resilient, responsive and respectful of others' time, and if you find someone who is willing to help, do not take it personally if what they share is not something you want to hear.

ALWAYS REMEMBER

The process of going from rucksack to briefcase can be challenging, but it is doable with courage, discipline, and little bit of help. As a service member, you already know the value of courage and discipline in achieving your goals. As a transitioning civilian-side employee, you'll need to learn the value of help.

Chapter 2
The Art of Transition

"Transition is not a one time thing. It is an on-going process. It is a re-learning. It is a recurring process. It can be repetitive. We can transition for years, and then suddenly find ourselves back at square one. Transition, especially after military service requires patience."—Chief Raymond

Getting Mentally Right

Now we are going to focus on what specifically needs to happen in order for you to go from rucksack to resumé. The first thing you need to know if you are separating from military service, being medically discharged or retiring is that you are *not* transitioning to the civilian work force, you are—first and foremost—returning back to the civilian sector. In other words, the transition is not simply about getting a job. It includes many other aspects of adjusting and re-adjusting from life in the military to life in the civilian sector.

Imagine, for a moment, that you are returning back to your old childhood neighborhood after being gone for many years. It is probably not the same and most certainly you are not the same. As a result, even though parts of it are familiar to you, you will need to figure out how to fit back in. This is the mental frame of mind I want you to have as we proceed.

In order to make a necessary point, let's go back in time to when you transitioned in the *other* direction—when you transitioned from the civilian sector *into* the military.

Take a few moments to think about the steps you had to go through as a young high school graduate, college student or, perhaps, someone who was working and wanted a new adventure in the military. So, you called Mr. Recruiter to get you processed.

If you did not have a family member or friend to give you some insight, you probably did not know what to expect. You had to take that in some cases painful 3½-hour Armed Services Vocational Aptitude Battery (ASVAB) entrance exam, then an all-day medical before finally earning a visit to speak with one of the guidance counselors.

You might have wanted to become a rocket scientist but were told your ASVAB results did not qualify you for the job. In all likelihood, if you decided to join, then right after basic training, you were assigned a job based on your skill set as well as on the needs of the branch of the military you joined. At that time, all you knew was how to be a civilian. You probably knew nothing about the military. You may have thought to yourself: *military people are so different*!

Now think about this. Did you expect the military to accept you, bad habits and all? Neither did they. That is why everyone goes through basic training no matter what branch of the military they join. They make sure that you are trained to understand and adhere to military standards, customs and courtesies, and that you understand what is expected of you.

In other words, you had to be taught what was necessary for you to survive and thrive in the armed forces. The military did not adjust to *you*. *You* had to adapt to the military if you wanted to be successful whether in a short or long career.

You were not born into the military. All you knew at the time was how to be a civilian. Once you decided to join the military you had to learn a new culture, adapt and apply yourself in order to be successful. Those who were not flexible, not willing, or not able to adapt to military culture were not successful.

Deployment for Employment

Now, your return to the civilian sector should be viewed in the same light. You will, in fact, have to learn a "new" culture, adapt and apply yourself in order to be successful. I cannot stress this enough. Never underestimate the degree to which you have changed as a result of your military service. People automatically assume that since civilian-side life is the norm, that "coming home" and resuming one's previous life should be the most natural thing one can do. However, you essentially had to become—or at least activate and hone—an entirely different person within you in order to survive and thrive within the unique reality of military service and perhaps combat. You now have to unlearn or "deactivate" that part of yourself in order to transition back. I'm not a psychologist, but I can tell you that military training and experience is profoundly mind-changing. Un-changing the uniquely designed military methods of turning you both mentally and physically into a fighting machine is not an easy task.

However, here is where that same military training and experience can give you an advantage to effect its own undoing—at least in the area of employment. As a service member, I want you to view this not simply as a return to civilian-side employment, but as a *deployment*. That's right. I want you to bring your "battle mind" to the challenge of finding a job. I want you to be resilient, and focused on the task as if you were deploying overseas into a combat zone. Of course, this is not combat, this is going to be your deployment to quality employment.

Also, when I say deployment, it should trigger in your mind that you have to do something, prepare, train and get ready for the unknown. Civilian-side, this means you start to find out as much as you can about the area you are deploying to, the people and culture. You assess your strengths, weaknesses and list all the opportunities and potential threats. You already have this training. Now you need to tweak and fine-tune it for civilian-side deployment!

Think about what happens in the military when you are competing for sailor, airman, marine, or soldier of the year award and recognition. How generous was your non-commissioned officer when it came to you meeting the individual qualifications for your annual physical test, weapons qualification or promotion boards? Probably not lenient at all, because it is *your* responsibility to prepare yourself for the task at hand. In fact, you will get mentored, counseled, or even disciplined if you do not meet those standards. Yes, shaped by the military, you're accustomed to challenges and of rising to meet and exceed them. Use that same courage and discipline when it comes to deploying for employment. Put in the extra work, earn the position, and do not look for someone to give you a job just for showing up.

In order to formulate your strategy, you have to take stock of yourself. On the next page is a simple inventory form to help.

You may not use all of this information, but having it in the forefront of your mind will be useful for our future exercises.

Personal Inventory

Name: _____

Branch of Service: _____

Military Occupational Skill/Rate: _____

Rank: _____

Duties and Responsibilities:
_____
_____
_____

Highest level of Command served:
_____

How large was your organization and how many people were served?
_____
_____

Your greatest accomplishments (be specific):
_____
_____

What are your strengths?
_____
_____
_____

What are your weaknesses?
_____
_____
_____

Notes:

Cultural Awareness Training

"You will usually be the most productive where you are the best fit."—Chief Raymond

This section will challenge you to think about and prepare for the type of culture in which you want to work; one in which you are comfortable and can thrive. First, however, let's start with the culture you are *leaving*, not just the branch of the military you are serving in, but all the way down the hierarchy to the unit level.

A shared set of values

Culture, as defined in the dictionary, is: *the set of shared attitudes, values, goals, and practices that characterizes an institution or organization.*

Think about it. There are unique attitudes, values, practices and environments within the unit you served, or are serving in—whether for good or bad—that you like or dislike. Use this knowledge as the basis to determine what you'll look for civilian-side. Do you like working in teams? What sorts of goals do you like to strive for? What is your attitude towards work and leisure? Do you prefer working alone in a private office or cubicle? Do you prefer professional or casual attire? Do you like working outdoors, turning a wrench, driving for a living, or providing security? This is not an all-inclusive list, but it will help you begin to clarify what's important to you when choosing your new work culture.

Now, you might be asking, with the job market the way it is, *Do I have a choice*? The answer is yes! Even though the job market may be difficult and people are *willing* to take what is available, *you* should strive to position yourself in the environment of your choice. Remember, you're going to be spending many hours of your day, and many days of the year in this position. You will usually be the most productive where you are the best fit.

Companies focus more on finding candidates who are a good fit, and whom they believe will do well in the culture of the organization more so than that candidate's skill set. Think about it for a minute. Why would I, as an employer, want to bring someone onto my team who—while she may be highly skilled as an individual—also comes with an attitude or personality that may damage the productivity of the team?

Now think about the military unit you are serving in. Imagine, for example, that in the area of physical fitness, your team currently has a high percentage of first time passing on the annual physical exam. Then, one day, a new service member joins the organization and—following his own set of attitudes, values, goals and practices—does not do what is necessary to pass the physical fitness test, and this results in an overall decrease in the team's effectiveness and their record. This new person may be okay or even good at his/her job, but not at contributing to the overall enhancement of the organization. How would that affect the team's morale? How will it affect how the team interacts with this new member? How much productive time will they lose thinking and gossiping about "the new guy" instead of focusing on the goals and tasks at hand?

Personal Appearance

Another important aspect of culture is your dress and appearance. In recent years, a unique trend of bodily adornment has become increasingly popular: tattoos and body piercing. I do not personally have anything against them, but they are (at least at this period in our society) simply not appropriate in most/all corporate cultures.

This is true in the military as well. Earrings are not appropriate for men in uniform. (Note: There are some instances—that vary per branch of service—when women *can* wear earrings when in uniform.) Tongue rings, lip rings, eye piercing and belly rings are prohibited in most cases on *and* off military duty. There is a standard in the wear of make-up and the color of nail polish while in uniform. The military has a standard for men's hair length, and how a woman's hair should be styled while in uniform.

A culture checklist

"*It takes far less effort to find and move to the culture that has what you want than it does to try to reconstruct an existing culture to match your standards.*" – adapted from a quote by Harry Browne, *How I Found Freedom in an Unfree World*

I've substituted the word "culture" in place of "society" in Harry Browne's quote, but the resulting quote still holds true. Whether you served six months, two years, or twenty, *you* adapted and changed to fit the culture of the military. By that same logic, do not expect a civilian-side company to change *its* culture and the way it operates to suit *you*. Instead, find companies that already have the type of culture you want to be a part of.

Decide which of these aspects of workplace culture are important to you and seek companies that offer what you want.

- *casual vs professional attire*
- *hair styles*
- *communication style*
- *overtime expectations*
- *personal expression (i.e. body art, piercings, jewelry)*
- *team vs individual*
- *flex-time vs rigid time*

Chapter 3
The Art of Communication

"You should not, cannot and must not alienate 99% of the population when you attempt to communicate, and more importantly, when you attempt to get a job."

Este capítulo es muy importante.

Dieses Kapitel ist sehr wichtig

Ceci est un chapitre très important dans ce livre.

이것은이 책에서 매우 중요한 장이다.

В этой книге есть важная глава.

在这本书中，这是一个非常重要的篇章。

Ito ay isang napakahalagang kabanata sa aklat na ito.

Sa a se yon chapit ki trè enpòtan nan liv sa a.

Hii ni sura muhimu sana katika kitabu hiki.

ذ. ەذا ەو فصل مەم جدا في ەذا الكتاب

Ito ay isang napakahalagang kabanata sa aklat na ito.

Great! With that vital bit of information out of the way, and now that I've gotten your attention, let's get started!

What's that? Come on now, I need you to keep up with me!

I know you've probably figured out where I'm going with this point, but please do not trivialize it. The purpose of this chapter is to help you overcome the eloquent language of acronyms you learned and perfected during your time of service. Your success in doing this will be vitally important in going from rucksack to briefcase.

I opened this chapter in Spanish, German, French, Korean, Russian, Chinese, Tagalog, Creole and Arabic (The sentence is: *"This is a very important chapter in this book."*) to make a simple point. Even if you speak many languages, it is likely there was something on that page you did not understand, and the way you looked at the strange, unfamiliar characters and the way you felt as you tried to gain understanding is exactly how employers, coworkers, family members and friends feel when you dazzle them with the large arsenal of acronyms you have become proficient in during your time of service. Do not expect everyone you come in contact with to understand our acronyms. In fact, practically no one civilian-side has any idea what you're talking about!

We use "ETS," "ACAP," etc. These are all foreign words to anyone who has not served in the military—in other words, to 99% of the population. You should not, cannot, and must not alienate 99% of the population when you communicate, and more importantly, when you're attempting to get a job. Here are a few reasons to take this seriously:

It is disrespectful

Communicating in a foreign language to someone you know does not understand it is rude and disrespectful. And yes, you *do* know they do not understand it because you yourself did not understand it before you joined the military, so how can *they*?!

People "tune out"

Beyond the basic courtesy of adjusting your language so others can understand you, there is an even more compelling reason to do so. Experts in the science of study techniques and comprehension have shown that people "tune out" when they encounter a word they do not understand. In other words, the human mind shuts down, and less additional information is processed when it encounters an undefined word. Experts say that all failure to complete any new course of study is caused by the individual coming across and failing to get the correct definition of the undefined word. In other words, the reason you always felt Physics was too difficult while in school, was because early on in the lessons or in the textbook, you came across a single word you didn't understand—and that no one ever fully explained—that crippled forever your future grasp of the subject. In the same way, when you are communicating with your prospective employer (or friend, neighbor or family member, for that matter) and you use a military acronym—a foreign, undefined word for them—they stop processing what you are saying. They tune out. Your words are no longer getting through. You are failing at communicating with them. You are failing *them* at understanding you. They are failing *you* like a physics test! Whose fault will it be if you do not get the job you are seeking? Who wants to hire and work with someone they cannot understand?

While reading the opening paragraph of this chapter you experienced the effect *your* words have when you speak in acronyms. Empathize with how others feel when you address them in military-speak and make the supreme effort to reprogram yourself for speaking civilian-side.

So now then, I want you to come to the position of attention, execute a right face, pick up a jog then go into a sprint. I am about to take you on a TDY trip, where you will do a PMCS of your language, get your annual PHA, do an AAR* and finally receive your Permanent Change of Language orders! This is a good time for us to coin, but never use this new acronym—PCL (Permanent Change of Language)—to help us define our goal as we transition into speaking to be understood civilian-side!

Translation Guide--Making the Change

Truthfully, I must admit, that as a former military person, when I take a call from another prior service member to pre-qualify them for one of our job openings, it is music to my ears to hear "our" language. They start rattling off acronyms one after the other as if they are giving a mission brief or providing me with grid coordinates and mission rendezvous points. It's as if I've returned to a unique place of comfort as a result of our shared experience. But then, I too have to snap out of it and remember that I, too, must get beyond that habit and determine if the candidate really has the skills I am looking for to fill my vacancies.

The prior service members who reach *my* office are fortunate they will be speaking to someone who is fluent in military-speak. However, what is the probability that *you* will get someone on the other end of the phone who will understand the words coming out of *your* mouth?

Translation:
TDY= *temporary duty when away from your location for at least a day.*
PMCS=*preventive maintenance check on equipment prior to use*
PHA= *an annual physical checkup service members are required to do*
AAR=*After Action Review is a summary conducted after each event to identify what was supposed to happen? i.e... Take the hill. What actually happened? What 3 things we did good? What 3 things can we do better?*

So after listening to and enjoying them drop a few acronyms for old times sake, I interject and ask them to clarify what they mean exactly when they say "TDY," "PCS," or "ETS. Its always interesting and sometime entertaining to listen to a bit of stumbling as they try to explain!

The key to communicating effectively and having a successful interaction with a civilian employer is knowing how our acronyms translate into civilian-speak. Here are few examples along with some simple scripts.

Old: "I am applying for this company because I am *ETS'ing* soon."
Translation: *ETS =Expiration Term of Service = end of contract*
New: "The reason I am applying with this company for the position of _____ is because my contract obligation is coming to an end after 2, 3, 4....20 years of successful service and I am looking at my options for how I can apply my skills in _____ to a new organization."

Old: "I'm considering your firm because I am *PCS'ing* to the area."
Translation: *PCS - Permanent Change of Station = relocation*
New: "I relocated to this area a few years ago to fill a career broadening assignment. My most recent assignment has provided me with the experience that would make me a direct fit for the position that you are currently trying to fill. I am now considering your company after researching several companies in this field."

Old: "I worked at several *FOB's* while deployed."
Translation: *FOB = Forward Operating Bases = training locations*
New: "I worked at several geographically disbursed training locations while deployed."

Old: "Where is the *mess hall/chow* hall located in this area?"
Translation: *mess hall = restaurant; cafeteria; dining hall*

Old: "Would you like a copy of my last 3 years of NCOER/OER?"
Translation: *Non-Commissioned/Officer Evaluation Report = evaluation*
New: "Would you like a copy of my performance evaluations for the past 3 years? I was evaluated annually by my immediate supervisor, as well as my supervisor's superior. The supervisors highlight my successes in areas of leadership, responsibility and my potential for promotion. The supervisors also make recommendation of areas that need improvement, if applicable."
NCOER = the report card for a non-commissioned officer enlisted service member (sergeant and above)
OER = the report card for all officers and warrant officers (lieutenants to Generals)

Old: "My MOS is Motor Vehicle Operator. My Rate is Electrician."
Translation: *MOS/Rate - Military Occupational Skill is the particular job you are trained for. In the Navy it is called rate. = training/profession*
New: "I was trained as a Motor Vehicle Operator. My military position is Electrician."

Old: "Where is the Latrine/Head located?"
Translation: *bathroom/restroom (*This should be an easy fix!*)*
New: "Where is the bathroom/men's room/ladies room, please?"

Old: "I have to check my LES to see how many days I've accumulated."
Translation: *Leave & Earnings Statement = pay stub*
New: "I will take a look at my pay stub to see how many days of vacation I've earned."

"I worked in…
Old: …G1 Section."
New: Human Resources Department for Personnel matters.

Old: …G2 Section"
New: Intelligence and Security Department

Old: …G3 Section"
New: Operations and Training Department

Old: …G4 Section"
New: Equipment and Logistics Support Division

Old: …G6 Section"
New: Communications and Information Technology Department

Old: …G8 Section"
New: Finance department

Old: "I start *Terminal Leave on June 1st."
New: "My transitional leave starts in June 1st."

Prior to separation or retirement from the military, a member may take the remainder of the leave they have accumulated. For instance, if a member's separation or retirement date is June 30, and the member has 30 days of leave accrued, the member may go on "terminal leave" beginning June 1st. Once they began "terminal leave" they would essentially be out of the military, but would still collect a paycheck and other entitlements, such as basic allowance for housing, basic allowance for subsistence and medical coverage until their official separation or retirement date on June 30.

Here are two additional examples that will come in handy in the chapter on interview skills.

Old: *Responses of agreement/understanding*
"Roger...I graduated from high school."
"Affirmative. I moved to this area about two years ago."
"Negative .I feel more comfortable in an entry-level position"
"Say it again over."
"Check!"

New: *Translations*
- I understand what you are saying.
- Yes, I graduated from high school
- Yes I moved to this area about two years ago
- No, I feel more comfortable starting in an entry-level position
- Would you mind repeating the last question, please?
- Thank you for your time, I look forward to speaking with you.

It is easier to "civilianize" your communication when you know the meanings of the acronyms and their equivalent context when speaking to someone in the civilian sector. Hopefully, after reading this chapter you'll be aware of your language, unlearn the old ways and reprogram yourself so you are clearly understood. Practice. Practice. Practice. I want it to be like muscle memory when you feel, hear or see yourself in a situation with the urge to lapse into military-speak. My goal is to give you a keen awareness so that you can adjust in action. If you get your mind wrapped around this skill you will be leaps and bounds ahead of the rest.

Tip: *ask your friends and relatives to let you know whenever you lapse into military-speak around them.*

ALWAYS REMEMBER
Effective communication is the key to success.

Chapter 4
Your Resumé

Your Resumé

The purpose of your civilian-side resumé is to tell the story about what you have done and what you can potentially do. It is your introduction to the civilian-side recruiter or hiring manager. It is no different than the officer's evaluation or enlisted/non-commissioned officer's evaluation usually requested when you apply for a certain position in your respective branch of service.

There are several resumé formats. The "correct" format depends on your background, and type of position you are applying for (i.e. government, private industry, non-profit, sales, etc.)

DO not—I repeat: DO NOT—be a resumé junkie! In other words, do not become addicted to creating "the perfect resumé." There is no such thing! I recommend creating two different versions, then start applying for jobs. Then, judge how "perfect" your resumé is by how many callbacks you receive. If recruiters are calling you back for interviews, that means there is something on the resumé that is catching their attention. That is the criterion for perfection. It's not the layout or the format. It's not even the grammar or your perfect spelling. No, the perfect resumé is one that speaks the recruiter-employer's language and gives him/her the idea that you just might be the one they are looking for!

If you grasp that single distinction, then you'll realize, therefore, that the next most important thing to remember is this:

A RESUMÉ DOES NOT GET YOU A JOB, A RESUMÉ SIMPLY PIQUES INTEREST IN ORDER TO GET YOU AN INVITATION FOR AN INTERVIEW!!!!!!

What *does, in fact,* ultimate "get" the job is your interview performance. Let's focus, then, on how to increase your chances of getting invitations for interviews. Some of these may seem obvious and basic, but it is often in overlooking the obvious and basic that we miss the critical path to achieving our goals.

Know what is on your resumé:

A few years ago, I was interviewing a candidate and asked him to tell me what the daily duties and responsibilities were at a company he worked. His answer was, "Oh, it's on my resumé." This was a "red flag" for me. As the recruiter, I already *knew* what was in his resumé. I was merely giving him an opportunity to show and shine, add some more details and sell himself. It was obvious however, that the candidate *himself* did not know what was on his resumé! My advice: if you have someone else write your resumé, then at least read and memorize it before your interview!

Be brief

As a recruiter, I can usually scan a resumé in 20-30 seconds looking for key words to determine if I should call a candidate for a telephone interview. I once had a candidate submit a Power Point® resumé that I thought was quite creative and quite entertaining with words flying in and fading out. However, all those bells and whistles took up way too much of my time. If he does not change his resumé to be concise and quantitative, he will, sadly, remain unemployed. Remember, the average recruiter has to browse many resumés to find potentially qualified candidates. Be sharp, crisp, concise and error free so he or she is compelled to stop when they get to your resumé.

Choose the best layout

There are two basic resumé layouts: chronological and functional. A chronological resumé emphasizes your job history over time, while a functional resumé emphasizes your skill set. There is a third type that is a blend of both.

Proofread your resumé

It's best to have others proofread your resumé. Sloppy resumé = sloppy job performance.

Get feedback and input

Have two or three people you respect provide some constructive feedback on the format and content of your resumé. These should be individuals who have hiring experience, or who have used their own resumés to secure employment. Take their advice as constructive feedback, but do not automatically make drastic changes as a result of their feedback if will change the unique story you wish to tell about yourself.

Start applying for jobs

A resumé isn't a resumé until it is being read by someone in a position to call you for an interview or follow-up

Tweak as necessary and continue submitting

Earlier, I suggested that you start submitting two different versions of your resumé. A resumé is an organic thing. In other words, it is (or should be) constantly evolving. Being able to assess which format and content is generating more interest is essential to knowing changes, additions and deletions might be necessary to improve your success going from rucksack to briefcase.

Key elements of your resumé

Here, now, are some tips and suggestions for the actual layout and content of your resumé. We'll start with the top half of the page. This is what the recruiter is going to see first and is, therefore, the most important "real estate" of your resumé!

Name and address

Your name and address should be clear and up to date.

Email address

If you include an email address, my recommendation is to use a separate professional email account (Gmail, Hotmail and Yahoo are all free) that you check on a regular basis. Remember, you only have one chance to make a professional first impression. Do not include your nickname or prior military field, especially if it is combat related. Here are a few examples of what NOT to use:

Expertsniper2013@   *whosyourdaddy01@*
Navysealsteam@   *pookieandmike@*
oneshotonekill@   *infantryman82confirmed@*
armyrangerhooah@   *goingpostal7910@*
airassaultonbeleigh@   *pimpdaddybubba@*

If you want to use these types of email addresses for personal use that's fine. For job-hunting, however, use a combination of your first name or initial and last name. Here are two examples of how you might wish to set up your email.

First name.last name@
First initial.last name@

Remember the professionalism you displayed during your military career and demonstrate it always.

Contact Number

Make sure your resumé provides a working contact number. I cannot tell you how many times I've called a number only to discover it was disconnected. If necessary, get yourself a separate pre-paid cell phone you can use for career opportunities.

Use a short, professional voice mail message. Now, don't get me wrong, I *love* music and motivational sayings, but if you are looking for employment, that sort of voicemail embellishment may not be appropriate. Also, do not play jokes on your voicemail (eg. *"Hello? Hello? Aaah, got ya! I am not available to take your call...."*) The caller may not appreciate your choice of music, motivation, or your winning sense of humor!

Objective Statement

The most important element after the contact information is your objective statement, or professional summary.

I do not particularly like objective statements unless they are for a specific position—i.e., *"my objective is to be a doctor, attorney, police officer."* (It will help if you include the specific company name.) I see a lot of "cookie cutter" objective statements about wanting "to join a company that is growing, appreciates my skills and yadda, yadda yadda." That's simply too generic and doesn't help a recruiter who is trying to figure out what position you are actually applying for. Remember, the recruiter is interested in finding quantifiable, measurable criteria for how you contributed to previous organizations. This helps them assess how you can help their company *make* money through your creative/technical skills and experience, or *save* money through the safety and efficiency of your processes. You can usually cover this in a professional summary highlighting your soft skills.

What not to include

Once past the top half of the page, we focus now on the content. *What information should I put on my resumé? What should I leave off the resumé?* Here are a few things not to include:

1) Marital Status
2) Gender
3) Religion
4) Birthday/Age
5) Photo (acceptable outside the US, when writing a CV)
6) Hobbies
7) References
8) Race
9) Place of Birth/Citizenship
10) How many children you have
11) Nickname
12) GPA
13) Hours worked
14) Salary
15) "Candidate for/expected completion" for college degree

None of these are relevant to your qualifications for the position you are applying for. However, once an offer is made, you may be required to provide additional information to complete the employment process.

A word about employment gaps

Be prepared to explain gaps in employment especially if there have been gaps of more than two years between jobs. Now, you have every right to do what you wish with your time, and there's no law that says you have to work continuously, all the time for your entire life. However, the people reviewing your resumés have to be certain they know important details about what you've been up to. Think about it, an unexplained gap of two years or more could mean you were in jail! While it might be unfair for them to use that against you, it is valuable information they need to know. In any case, whatever the reason for your employment gaps, don't be *afraid* to answer the question just be *prepared* to answer it. If you were in school, or if you were traveling the world, then say that and be sure to explain what you gained from that experience—more knowledge, skills, etc. If you stayed home for a period of time to take care of an ill family member, then say that, but focus on what things you did while you were home: *"I volunteered at the local YMCA, read books to learn more about my area of expertise, joined a professional organization so I stayed up to date on the current practices in my field."* or *"I was a stay at home father for a short two years after separating from active duty. During that period of time, I took the time to complete my Associates degree. I joined the Army Reserves where I earned some additional funds, and maintained some relevant experience."*

Do not try to "stretch" the dates on your resumé to prevent the appearance of gaps. Be truthful and transparent. Hiring managers look for "fluff" and gaps in the resumé.

White space

It is okay to leave some "white space" on the page. Do not list everything that you have ever done or try to squeeze it all on one page. That could work against you. By putting too much information in your resumé, (a) you have told the company everything they need to know about you and so there is no need to interview *you*; and (b) it is too much work and words for the recruiter to wade through to find what you have done, what your accomplishments are, and what you want to do.

The Length of the RESUMÉ

The "correct" length of your resumé depends upon your experience. A candidate with ten or more years of experience will do an injustice to herself if she tries to squeeze everything into a one-page document with Times New Roman font size 8! It's perfectly acceptable to have a two-page resumé, but not much more.

If you are transferring from the federal employment to the private sector, re-work your resumé and include only the most relevant information. I once had a potential candidate submit a resumé disguised as an eleven-page novel that wore me out to review! My mind shut down after the first page!

If you have a resumé company do your resumé make sure you have some input. You want to know what is in your resumé. I had a company do a resumé for me and they simply took all the information I had given them and dropped it into their template to create a three-page resumé. Ultimately, I wondered why I was getting no calls with this professionally made resumé. It was simply too overwhelming, and recruiters had to really work in order to read and decipher the meat from the potatoes.

Final Words

Remember, your resumé will not *get* you a job. The resumé's purpose is to pique an employer's interest in the hopes of getting a callback to appear for an interview. During the interview is where you'll demonstrate you are the best candidate.

Do not—and I repeat, *do not*—delay your future success by attempting to create a perfect resumé before you start sending it out and applying for jobs.

Keep in mind, as well, that your resumé is being viewed by humans who have different perspectives and tastes. However, the bottom line question they seek to answer remains the same: *What is your benefit to and fit within the company?*

Now, I want you to get in character and imagine *you* are a recruiter, hiring manager or business owner and that you are reviewing a stack of resumés from candidates just like you applying for a job. Here is the first question you need to ask after viewing your own resumé:

Would you call yourself in for an interview? Why?
Is it because, based on the resumé,
a. You seem like a really nice person
b. You meet the minimum qualifications; seem best qualified?
c. You used the correct font, spacing and quality paper?
d. You wrote: "*I am a hard worker, arrive on time & trustworthy*"

If the reason is anything other than "b," you need to adjust your resumé so that you clearly articulate your background and experience. On the other hand, if you can honestly recognize your resumé does not offer a compelling reason to hire you, then do not expect a company to hire you either! Back to the drawing board!

For the record, if you really believe "d" is good reason to hire someone, then I've got news for you: being a hard worker who arrives on time is what's expected! It's what you bring to the table *beyond* the basics that will get you a callback!

Let's get to work on your resumé

It's often said that the best way to learn something is to teach it to someone else. Similarly, the best way for you to learn how to create an effective resumé is to teach someone how to do it for him/herself. The goal of this section is for you to pretend you are teaching someone how to write a better resumé. Review and list all the things you believe may be wrong or that could be improved about these two resumés. Then compare your findings and suggestions with mine!

PAGE 1 OF ORIGINAL RESUMÉ

> **Johnny Service Member**
> 10225 Mockingbird Lane, Ready, AZ 54321
> Cell: 987-654-3210
> Email: hardcharging@gmail.com
>
> **Profile:**
> Dedicated professional with 20 years of outstanding performance in the U.S. Army earning the rank of Sergeant First Class and have excelled as a leader. Accountable and ambitious, able to remain focused and productive in challenging situations. Trained and mentored countless soldiers through difficult situations. Vast knowledge in electrical theory, troubleshooting procedures, soldering techniques, electrical system maintenance, and ability to read and follow electrical schematics.
>
> **Military Experience:**
> **September 2007–August 2013 (6 years 0 months) CSJFTC**
> Responsible for enforcing all safety and operations procedures for Ranges, Training Areas, and Training Facilities for all branches of the military that are deploying and attending regular training events. Organized schedule for 20 soldiers, successfully enhancing time efficiency.
>
> **2001-Current   18th TASMG Ft. Jackson, SC**
> Key positions include Platoon Sergeant, Squad Leader and Technical Inspector on AH64-D Apache Helicopters. During each stint in charge of an average of 20 personnel. Served as a Technical Inspector as well as in charge of all armament maintenance on all attack helicopters. Deployed to Iraq from November 2005-July 2006.
>
> **1996-2001 17th Airborne Division, Ft. Hamilton, NY**
> Key positions include Platoon Sergeant and Squad Leader in charge of 15 personnel and all armament and electrical maintenance on 8 aircraft. Signed for and accountable for the safety of over $5 million in equipment and parts. Deployed to Bosnia from September 1999-April 2000.
>
> **1992-1996 5th Infantry Division, Ft. Drum, NY**
> Key positions as team leader in charge of specific tasks of aircraft maintenance to include daily and phase operations.
>
> **1992-Present**
> Diagnose, troubleshoot and repair electrical malfunctions in the AH-64D systems and components. Maintain and authorize modifications to weapons components, fire control units, sighting elements, electronic and mechanical devices. Perform operational and preventive checks. Maintain records on weapons and subsystems.

YOUR NOTES FOR IMPROVING PAGE 1 OF RESUMÉ:
How would you advise Johnny to improve this page of his resumé?

Section 1-Profile:
a) _____
b) _____
c) _____
d) _____
e) _____

Section 2-Military experience:
a) _____
b) _____
c) _____
d) _____
e) _____

Section 3-Civilian Experience:

a) _____
b) _____
c) _____
d) _____
e) _____
f) _____
g) _____
h) _____
i) _____
j) _____
k) _____
l) _____
m) _____
n) _____
o) _____
p) _____

PAGE 2 OF ORIGINAL RESUMÉ

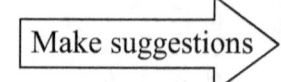

Civilian Experience:

2002-2005 The Motorcycle Store (3 years 0 months)
Responsible for product assembly, in-home customer evaluation and training, product delivery and service of power chairs, scooter, and lifts.

Civilian Education:

High School Diploma – Marine Academy, Mandatory, WY
Forty-Six semester hours at Johnson Community College, Watertown, NY

Military Education:

Basic Training- Ft. Dix, NJ
Primary Leadership Development Course- Fort Dix, NJ
Basic Non-Commissioned Officers Course- Fort Dix, NJ
Level 2 Range Safety School- Camps Parks, CA
Aircraft Armament/Electrical/Avionics Systems Repairer School- North Pole,

Awards/Medals:

Army Commendation Medal: 7
Army Achievement Award: 4
Numerous other awards

Note: References available upon request.

YOUR NOTES FOR IMPROVING PAGE 2 OF RESUMÉ:
How would you advise Johnny to improve this page of his resumé?

Section 4-Civilian Education:

a) _____
b) _____
c) _____
d) _____
e) _____

Section 5-Military Education:

a) _____
b) _____
c) _____
d) _____
e) _____

Section 6-Army Awards:

a) _____
b) _____
c) _____
d) _____
e) _____

Section 7-References:

a) _____
b) _____
c) _____
d) _____
e) _____

How well do you think you did? Let's compare your notes to mine to see if we both caught the same things.

Chief Raymond's Corrections Page 1

Johnny Servicemember
1313 Mockingbird Lane, Ready, AZ 54321
Cell: 987-654-3210
Email: hardcharging@gmail.com — a. unprofessional email

b. Rank not necessary

Profile: ← f. remove or justify

Dedicated professional with 20 years of outstanding performance in the U.S. Army earning the rank of Sergeant First Class and have excelled as a leader. Accountable and ambitious, able to remain focused and productive in challenging situations. Trained and mentored countless soldiers through difficult situations. Vast knowledge in electrical theory, troubleshooting procedures, soldering techniques, electrical system maintenance, and ability to read and follow electrical schematics. — d. Vague

c. rephrase passive

g. change to Work Experience **Military Experience:**

e. last sentence should be first

September 2007–August 2013 (6 years 0 months) CSJFTC — h. What is this????
Responsible for enforcing all safety and operations procedures for Ranges, Training Areas, and Training Facilities for all branches of the military that are deploying and attending regular training events. Organized schedule for 20 soldiers, successfully enhancing time efficiency.

i. Months not necessary   j. What is this????

2001-Current 18th TASMG Ft. Jackson, SC
Key positions include Platoon Sergeant, Squad Leader and Technical Inspector on AH64-D Apache Helicopters. During each stint in charge of an average of 20 personnel. Served as a Technical Inspector as well as in charge of all armament maintenance on all attack helicopters. Deployed to Iraq from November 2005-July 2006.   k. what is a "Platoon Sergeant?"

1996-2001 17th Airborne Division, Ft. Hamilton, NY
Key positions include Platoon Sergeant and Squad Leader in charge of 15 personnel and all armament and electrical maintenance on 8 aircraft. Signed for and accountable for the safety of over $5 million in equipment and parts. Deployed to Bosnia from September 1999-April 2000.

l. Be consistent in use of terminology

1992-1996 5th Infantry Division, Ft. Drum, NY
Key positions as team leader in charge of specific tasks of aircraft maintenance to include daily and phase operations.

1992-Present
Diagnose, troubleshoot and repair electrical malfunctions in the AH-64D systems and components. Maintain and authorize modifications to weapons components, fire control units, sighting elements, electronic and mechanical devices. Perform operational and preventive checks. Maintain records on weapons and subsystems.

CHIEF RAYMOND'S NOTES FOR PAGE 1

Section 1-Profile:
a. Unprofessional email address
b. Rank is irrelevant in the profile
c. *Able to remain focused* is a passive statement. Rephrase (eg. focused and challenge-driven leader.)
d. *Mentored countless Soldiers*- Vague statement. Do not quantify accomplishments in profile.
e. Last sentence should be the first. *Vast* is vague (eg. *Subject matter expert in electrical theory*)
f. Remove "Army" from profile unless you can justify how including it will increase your chances of getting the interview
Additional: Use this section for strategic, analytical and project management skills as well as teamwork and communication.

Section 2-Military experience:
g. Think like a civilian. Title this section "work experience." Is it necessary to indicate whether it is civilian or military?
h. What on earth does CSJFTC mean????? I am a civilian.
i. Not necessary to list the months you've been at a job.
j. What is TASMG?
k. What is a Platoon Sergeant or Squad Leader? Think civilian.
l. The jobs do not flow smoothly in a chronological order.

Additional: Include quantitative successes (what process was improved, how much money did you save the company?) Include scope of responsibility (i.e. who/what/how many you managed; where were you geographically located?)

Additional: Place job descriptions in chronological order starting with the most recent (based on end date).

Additional: You deployed twice? Great. So what? Assume the person reviewing this knows nothing about the military or what you do. Before you include something like a deployment in your resumé, ask, "How will this add value to my chances of getting an interview?" Save the deployment discussion for the interview and/or/if you are asked a behavioral question. (eg. *Give an example of a time where you had [X] happen. What did you do?)*

Chief Raymond's Corrections Page 2

m. Again, use single category: "Work Experience"

n. Not needed

Civilian Experience:

2002-2005 (3 years 0 months) The Motorcycle Store
Responsible for product assembly, in-home customer evaluation and training, product delivery and service of power chairs, scooter, and lifts.

Civilian Education:

o. Create single education categ.

High School Diploma – Marine Academy, Mandatory, WY
Forty-Six semester hours at Johnson Community College, Watertown, NY

Military Education:

p. What about Secondary course?
q. What's a Non-commissioned Officer

Basic Training- Ft. Dix, NJ
Primary Leadership Development Course- Fort Dix, NJ
Basic Non-Commissioned Officers Course- Fort Dix, NJ
Level 2 Range Safety School- Camps Parks, CA
Aircraft Armament/Electrical/Avionics Systems Repairer School- North Pole,

r. Is Level 1 better than Level 2?
s. List and simplify this course

Awards/Medals:

t. What's this? Is it applicable?

Army Commendation Medal: 7
Army Achievement Award: 4
Numerous other awards

u. What's this? Is it relevant?
v. Vague.

Note: References available upon request.

w. Not necessary to say

CHIEF RAYMOND'S NOTES FOR PAGE 2

Section 3-Civilian Experience:
m. All work experience should be listed as "work experience."
n. Not necessary to list the years and months worked.
Additional: Quantify, quantify! How many pounds, pieces or dollars were involved? Were you the top producer in your store/region? How much product was delivered, in what period?

Section 4-Civilian Education:
o. Create single "Education" section
Additional: List completed courses with degree or certification

Section 5-Military Education:
p. Is there a "Secondary" course? Which one is better?
q. What is a non-commissioned officer?
r. What is level 2-range safety course? That will open up other questions. Did the person complete Level 1-safety school? How does the course correlate with the job applied for? Keep it simple.
s. List the exact title of the aircraft course. Could the position/title be simplified as "aircraft mechanic?"

Section 6-Army Awards:
t. What is an Army commendation medal? How does it apply and add value to the job applied for?
u. What is an Army Achievement Award? How does it apply to the qualifications of the applied for position?
v. Numerous other awards- Vague statement again how does it apply and add value to the position applied for?

Additional: Do not list on the resumé if it does not add value. You may consider adding an item if it shows your diversity or other qualifications that may be of potential value (other languages, computer skills/specific software, physical fitness, etc.)

Section 7-References:
w) The job application will ask you to list references, so it is not necessary to include in the resumé.

Chief Raymond's revised "Rucksack to Briefcase" Resumé:

Johnny Servicemember
10225 Marking Bird Lane, Ready, AZ 54321
Cell: 987-654-3210
Email: j.servicemember@gmail.com

PROFESSIONAL SUMMARY

Results-oriented Electrical Avionics Technician with more than 20 years experience. Challenge driven leader able to overcome complex technical issues and deliver results. Strong troubleshooting and analytical skills. Out the box thinker with a proactive approach to safety and maintenance. Skilled communicator and facilitator with project management multi-task skills.

Professional Experience:

September 2007–August 2013, Joint Training Center, Camp Shelby, MS
- Safety Professional in charge of 10 ranges, covering 50 acres.
- Trained more than 10k Service members annually, with zero accidents
- Served as Human Resource Manager for a Staff of 20. Responsible for training and professional development and daily activity of the staff.
- Maintained 100 % accountability of more than 1 million rounds of ammunition annually.

2002-2005 The Motorcycle Store
- Served a product assembler, assembling more 10k pounds, 50k dollars of product
- Delivered and assembled more than 30k dollars worth of product

2001-2002 18th Aviation Sustainment Maintenance Group Ft. Jackson, SC
- Technical inspector for 60 Apache helicopters.
- Developed new standard operating procedure for maintenance of 60-Apache helicopters
- Served as Human Resource Manager for a Staff of 20. Responsible for training and professional development and daily activity of the staff.
- Maintained 100 % accountability of sensitive items and supplies for Apache helicopter

1996-2001 17th Airborne Division, Ft. Hamilton, NY
- Subject matter expert on the upkeep and maintenance of 8 aircrafts.
- Custodian for more than 5 million dollars worth of equipment and parts
- Human Resource Manager for a Staff of 15 for training and professional development and daily activity of the staff.
- Served as unit safety manager

1992-1996 5th Infantry Division, Ft. Drum, NY
- Subject matter expert on the upkeep and maintenance of 10 aircrafts.
- Human Resource Manager for a Staff of 10 for training and professional development and daily activity of the staff.

Education:
High School Diploma – Marine Academy, Mandatory, WY
Initial Training- Ft. Dix, NJ
Primary Leadership Development Course- Fort Dix, NJ
Advanced Leadership Course- Fort Dix, NJ
Range Safety Training- Camps Parks, CA
Electrical Aircraft Avionics Systems Repair Course- North Pole,

Lost in Translation? Not anymore!

Now, wasn't that fun? As you can see, the challenge in translating your military service into civilian-speak is in understanding the scope of work of the military positions you have held (i.e. people served, size of the organization, responsibilities, etc.), and finding alternate terminology someone in the civilian sector will understand. Here are a few suggestions to help translating your resumé into civilian-speak:

Military Terminology	Civilianized Terminology
Company	Business unit
Platoon	Business unit
Section	Department
Command Staff	Executive Staff
"I supervised soldiers, marines, airmen"	"I supervised a staff of 10 people..."
Brigade, Battalion Headquarters	Corporate Office
Platoon Sergeant, 1st Sergeant	Manager, supervisor
US Army, Marines, Air Force, Navy, Coast Guard, Military	Department of Defense
Senior NCO	Assistant Manager, Senior Manager

Remember, for the majority of the world's population, military experience represent a different reality, a foreign language and a hidden operation with a unique set of job titles, scopes of work, objectives and skill sets that are not easily translatable into exact civilian-side counterparts.

"Highlighting your military experience to secure a civilian-side job is like coming to earth from another planet, for instance, and listing all the things you did on Rigel VII without allowing for the fact that no one on earth has been there, speaks the language or appreciates your home planet's contribution to the Federation of Planets."—**Chief Raymond, Star Trek fan**

Chapter 5
Job Hunting

Chief Ray, I've got my resumé! Now what????

Now that you have a re-engineered, top of the line, quality resumé, what do you do next?

Well, hopefully, you've already figured out what you want to do as a career (industry, field), what hours (part-time or full-time), what type (private, public, government, non-profit) and size of company you want to work for. The next step is to begin putting the word out that you're looking for a job, and begin distributing your resumé. It's time to start job hunting!

The first thing I want to let you in on is: This is a numbers game! In other words, the greater the number of resumés you submit to the right people, the more success you will eventually have. Notice I said, "the right people." You should make sure your resumé is getting into the right hands…many of the right hands!

Return on Investment

Before you get started, however, you need to have system to evaluate your return on investment. When I say "return on investment," I am talking about how many callbacks you receive after submitting your resumé. This is how you measure the effectiveness of your resumé and the effectiveness of your strategy.

It may take a little time for the momentum of your efforts to reach critical mass. Just like pushing a car that is standing still, it takes a lot of initial effort to get things moving and in process. So, if you do not immediately start receiving callbacks, don't despair. It might simply be that the hiring officials have not had a chance to get around to all the people who have applied. However, if after a few months, you have established a routine of putting resumés out in the market place, applying for jobs, and are *still* not receiving callbacks, consider making slight revisions to your resumé. Callbacks are an indication your resumé is piquing interest.

Internet Job Hunting

Do not make the mistake of thinking that hunting for a job on the Internet will be a productive strategy. I know it *feels* good. You can sit at home in your pajamas filling out applications and submitting resumé after resumé with the click of a button. However, you want your resumé to get in the hands of the hiring officials, and you have no way of knowing if the right people are actually viewing it. If most of your time is spent searching via the Internet, I strongly suggest you shift that time. Here's why.

Many companies/services that accept online submissions, use systems that search those submissions for specific key words and/or phrases. If you don't have the right keywords in your resumé, you could be eliminated and effectively face another obstacle in reaching the right people involved in the hiring process. You see, once a company is on the Internet, virtually the entire world has access to applying for open jobs, and a company may have hundreds—if not thousands—of resumés to sort through. Where will yours end up?

I learned the answer to that question the hard way in my quest for a job. I created a resumé, and sent it out to a distribution company, hoping and praying someone would discover me amongst the other hundreds of resumés. Frustration set in. I did not want to continue the process. I would come home and put my head under the pillow not wanting to face reality. I felt like a loser, returning from deployment and not being able to find employment.

The Internet is the most comfortable yet least effective way to find a job. Sure, you may get lucky, but *people* are your best source and resource for landing a job, and that brings me to my patented 3-step strategy for going from rucksack to briefcase: Network! Network! And then, network some more!

Network! Network! Network!

The greatest and most effective source for finding out about jobs is usually word of mouth. Another word for it is networking. I've heard it said *"if you don't NETwork, there's a chance you will NOTwork!"* and as the popular saying goes, *"it's often not what you know but who you know, and what they know about you!"*

Often, when people think about networking, they think of it almost like having to campaign for political office. They imagine talking to strangers, shaking hands and kissing babies all in an effort to win people over and getting them to like you. They decide they don't like it, don't have the personality for it, or simply don't know how to do it effectively.

Well, networking is nothing more than simple communication between two or more people. The goal of that communication is to build and maintain professional and friendly relationships where you each have the opportunity to be resourceful to each other. The way you do that is simply by letting someone else know who you are, telling him/her what you are seeking, find out what *he/she* is seeking, and discussing ways you might help each other.

Think about how things were in military at the end of your first assignment. When it came time to look for your next assignment, you might have found someone you went to basic training with who now works in the area, base or fort you are considering. You might have asked if they knew someone there who—or if they themselves could—put in a word in for your to increase the chances of you getting the interview or position. That's all networking is. At times the successes may seem random, coincidence or plain luck, but it doesn't actually happen by accident. It happened because communicated your intentions and interests to someone else. Now, you simply have to be more conscious and more deliberate and intentional in doing so. You never know when you know someone who knows someone who knows someone, etc.

When to network

The best time to start networking and hunting for a job is NOW!!!!! Don't wait until a month before you are about to leave the service or you will find yourself already behind in the race. The best time to look for work is while you still have work! Think about it. If you are offered a new job while you're already employed, you can always turn it down if it's not good enough, and of course, you can always accept it. You won't be operating from a position of desperation where you're likely to accept the first offer you receive.

Volunteering

Another way to increase your networking circles is through volunteering. Consider volunteering in an area you think you might want to work in, and do so while you're still employed. Or better, yet, make a conscious effort to volunteer in an area you're passionate about, and build your network among people who are making money doing what *you* might really enjoy doing, too!

Network at Job Fairs:

Networking at job fairs is a great way to land a job. However, most people make the mistake of showing up at the job fair with out doing any research. You should:

1) find out what companies are going to be there ahead of time;
2) visit the company website to see what jobs are available;
3) approach each company with a specific plan.

Think back to the planning you used when going in on a four man stack to take a building. Each person had his assigned mission going in. Everyone knew who was breaching, who was leading and everything got done quickly, efficiently and expeditiously. "Get in, get on and get out!"

In order to help you do that civilian-side, it will help if you know what the business actually does, the products they sell, and the geographic locations they operate in. The bottom line question is "how does the company make money?" Businesses serve one main purpose, and that is to make money. If you understand how they make money you can paint a picture of how you plan to contribute to the bottom line.

Candidate A walks up to the recruiter at a local job fair and says, *"What does your company do? What positions are you recruiting for? Where are you located?"*

Candidate B walks up to the same recruiter and says, *"My name is Private Snuffy. I visited your website and saw that you are hiring for an Information Technology position. I am very interested. In fact, for the last four years I've been working in the field at various levels of my current organization. I see that my experience is a direct match for what you're looking for, and I am very interested in the position. Who is the hiring manager, and how soon is your company looking to fill this position?"*

Which candidate do you think will be the most successful at that job fair? That's right! Snuffy had a plan with a tight strategy that made a great impression on that recruiter. An impressed recuriter may take your resumé and even make notes to give directly to the hiring manager!

Social media networking

Social media (Facebook, Twitter, etc) are good ways of publicizing your job search and for marketing yourself. As you do so, however, I caution you to protect your "brand." Anything and everything that appears about you online is essentially advertising your brand identity to the world. Therefore, it is oh so important to understand that once you hit the send/post button on your Facebook account, or on the forum/bulletin board of that group you joined, it is difficult to completely clear and erase it. So, be extremely careful with whom you associate in the social arena

These days, when deciding whether to hire you, companies can and do typically check your social network. Now, *you* may not be saying negative or controversial things online, but the people *you associate with* and what *they* are saying and doing can influence how others view you. Remember, while job hunting, your resumé, as well as your social network are being assessed and judged by human beings with their own perceptions.

With that said, as far as online networks, I am a big fan of LinkedIn® (www.LinkedIn®.com) LinkedIn® is a professional networking site with over 225 million registered users, many resources as well as groups you can join and follow. As a recruiter, I use LinkedIn® to narrow my search criteria to pinpoint qualified candidates based on their profiles and summaries.

I recommend, therefore, that you create a LinkedIn® profile and a summary about yourself. Your profile need not read like a resumé, but if the profile is done correctly, recruiters and hiring managers like myself may find and prospect you. Some recruiters won't even work with you if you don't have a LinkedIn® account.

Keep in mind as well, that the more "connections" you have in your LinkedIn® network, the greater the chances of showing up on the radar of someone looking for prospects like you.

Start developing a network, connect and join groups with professionals, hiring authorities and people who are doing what you would like to do. The ultimate number of people in your network of connections can grow exponentially!

Now, we've all heard the theory of exponential growth: one person who tells 2 who tell 4 who tell 8, and within a few "generations," you're into the thousands! It makes for exciting reading, so I decided to test it for myself. I went on a several-month LinkedIn® "connection mission!" When it was all done, my personal connections grew from 130 to over 1,900 and that 1,900 now connect me to over 80,000 people in total!

LinkedIn® also has a cool "analytics" feature. It tells me:
1) who viewed my profile. If someone looked at my profile, I will look at theirs to determine if I want to connect with them;
2) how many times I came up in searches in the past three days
3) in what location and industry these searches occurred;
4) the actual search words that were used to find me in a search.

Tip: If someone requests a "connection" with you through LinkedIn®, do not immediately start asking about job openings. Thank them for the connection, and start to cultivate a conversation and a relationship. Do not approach networking with the "What's In It For Me" mentality. Employ a mutually beneficial, win-win strategy for your networking.

It wasn't like this in the military!!

Yes, I know. When you changed jobs in the military and reported to a new assignment, it was based on your job function, experience and rank. You did not have to submit a resumé or even interview in some cases. You may have been asked to provide your last three evaluations, a biography and a copy of your last physical fitness test scorecard, but no interview, no resumé, no interview questions and no salary negotiation. However, the fact that you never had to do before what the civilian sector requires you to do now does not alleviate you of the responsibility of getting it done!

The only constant in life is change. The great news for you is that as an ex or soon-to-be ex-military, you have the internal fortitude to persevere, to keep fighting and keep moving in the face of adversity, opposition *and* change!

Network by the Numbers

Here are a few additional tips for increasing the numbers:

Make a list of everyone you know

One of the first things I learned when I joined a sales and marketing team was to start with my "warm" market—the individuals with whom I have the most direct relationships.

Your first assignment is to sit and make a complete and thorough list of <u>every single person</u> you know directly or indirectly. Most people aren't aware that they actually know hundreds, perhaps thousands of people. Include uncles, friends of uncles you met at the Super Bowl party, neighbors, doormen, mail carriers; everyone should be on that list. Then, systematically let each and every one of them know you are in the middle of a job search. You can mention it in an email, or casually mention it the next time you meet them, but you must not consider yourself done until each and every person on that list has a check mark next to their name indicating they know you are on a quest. If they happen to mention someone they think might be of assistance to you, then add *that* person to your list, too, and follow up and follow through with that new person as well. There's no excuse for sitting idle. As long as there are people on that list, and as long as you don't have a job—or the job you want—you always have something to do!

Work for military...sort of

Even though you may be returning from active duty or deployment, there are administrative positions on military bases or military organizations for which you may be qualified.

Create a Youtube® interview video

Now, I've never personally used this approach, but it is creative. If I received a video resumé, I would definitely review it. Here are two I found online (not affiliated with me or my company).
http://www.Youtube®.com/watch?v=S2RlnDqI-JQ
http://www.Youtube®.com/watch?v=a2L9DGEUtNg

Add a note to your email signature file

For those of us who still use email to communicate, the signature file—(official term: valediction) that you can create and program to automatically appended to each outgoing email—can be a great way to communicate your job search with everyone.

>   ~~~~~~~~~~~~~~
>   *...Regards,*
>   *John Smith*
>   *(212) 345-6789*
>   *Currently seeking new opportunities in _____ industry*
>   **[or]**
>   *Transitioning professional _____ & former service member*
>   **[or]**
>   *Experienced accountant seeking new opportunity*
>   *Check out my Youtube® interview at http://www.Youtube®.com/a;lkdflk;*
>   ~~~~~~~~~~~~~~~~~~~~~~~~~

Attend military-friendly and other job fairs.
Here is a short list.

Recruit Military job fairs	www.recruitmilitary.com
Military.com	www.Military.com
Civilianjobs National Job Fairs	www.civilianjobs.com
Military Officers Jobs Opportunities	www.military-mojo.com
Hiring our Heroes	uschamber.com/hiringourheroes
Military Spouse Hiring Fair/Career Forum	www.securityclearanceexpo.com
Security Clearance Job Fair	www.securityclearanceexpo.com
Top Secret Clearance Expo	www.techexpousa.com
NCOA Career Expo	www.ncoausa.org

Register with as many professional organizations as possible

Professional organizations exist for just about every profession providing the opportunity to network with other professionals in your and related fields. Here are a few:

Association of Information Technology (AITP):	http://www.aitp.org
National Society of Professional Engineers	http://www.nspe.org
National Association of Sales Professionals	http://www.nasp.com
National Speakers Associations	http://nsaspeaker.org
National Military Intelligence Association	http://www.nmia.org
National Electrical Contractors Associations	http://www.necanet.org
American Society of Transportation and Logistics	http://www.astl.org
Professional Aviation and Maintenance Association	http://pama.org
Automotive Maintenance and Repair Association	http://amra.org
American Culinary Association	http://www.acfchefs.org
Society for Human Resource Management	http://www.shrm.org

Keep a log

Keep a log of where you applied and when you sent the resumé so you are not caught off guard when you get the callback!

Create your own similar log sheet using this as a guide

Date	Company & Position	Contact person	Result Version	Phone screening	Result	Interview	Result	Offer	Decline or Accept	Start Date	Remarks

This log can provide a good indication of how well you are doing. If used correctly, you can gain some valuable statistical and historical data that can help you identify the part of your strategy you may need to tweak or eliminate.

1) It will give you an average of how many resumés you need to submit to receive a call back

2) You can monitor the amount of offers you are receiving and if they are within your desired range and requirements.

If you are not receiving callbacks after submitting a significant number of resumés., you may want to get some feedback on improving your resumé.

If you are receiving callbacks, but no invitations for face-to-face interviews, you may need to improve your telephone interviewing skills.

If you are successful with telephone interviews, and receiving invitations for face-to-face but no hard offers, then you may need to work on your face-to-face interviewing skills.

Chapter 6
A Vital Q&A

A Vital Q&A for the job seeker/service members

Q; Why are service members not successful in the job search?
A: It is normally because you do not have a strategy. You should should formulate this strategy *before* you leave the service. Follow the sugestions in this book after you get clear on what type of position, field, company and culture you wish to pursue.

Q: Is it okay to leave a voicemail message for a hiring official?
A: Yes.

Q: What information should I leave?
A: Keep it short, but leave your name, a good contact number, the reason for your call (ie…..the position you are interested in) and list 2-3 of your strongest skills that are applicable to the position.

Q: Is it necessary to indicate that I am a veteran?
A: Not necessary, unless the position calls for a person with military experience. If you believe it will add value and increase the probability of getting a call-back, then by all means do so. If not, save it for the application or during the interview, and bring it up if something successful that you have done while in the military is relevant to a question you are asked.

Q: Can I ask a recruiter if she has a position suitable for my experience?
A: No. That would indicate you have not done enough research to see what positions are available. It may indicate you do not understand your own skills and how they are applicable to the company's objectives. Most companies have a webiste that lists their objectives, as well as the particulars jobs that are open along with the requirements. It's not the recruiter's job to match you with a position. You have to sell yourself!

Q: What is a video interview?
A: A video interview is a pre-recorded interview of your answering questions. It is not interactive but treat it as such. Get dressed as if you were going for a face to face interview. Make sure your background is appropiate. Keep noise down, television off, pets and children away, and please do not have someone in the picture helping you with your answers. That does not go over well. (Note: some companies are using Skype® for interviews.)

Q: Is networking mandatory? I am shy. I don't talk easily to others.
A: No, it is not mandatory. However, it increases your exposure to people who know people, who know people. It's about leveraging the efforts of others. You could do 100% of the effort yourself, or for example, have 10 people each doing 10%. NETwork or NOT work. Work smart instead of working hard The choice is yours.

Q: How long should my resumé be?
A: That depends on your work history and experience. If you are a recent graduate from college it will probably only be one page. However, if you have ten or more years experience, you most certainly will have more than one page. Toot your horn and let it be known to the market place what you have done. Use metrics, successes, improvements of processes and savings of money.

Q: How far back in time should my resumé go?
A: You typically do not list work experience more than ten years old unless there is something specific that you did 12, 15 or 20 years ago that is applicable to the position you are currently applying for. The purpose of the resumé is to pique interest. It should get to the point without telling your entire life story. You do not want to present a lengthy resumé of more than two pages if you can help it unless you are applying for a government position.

Q: How detailed should each job description be?
A: A good format to use is to itemize your job description by bullet points, and let the length of time you worked at a position determine how many bullet points you use for that position.

For example if you were at a job for six months, then you are probably not going to have 6, 7 or 8 bullet points or significant impacts unless the job was highly specialized. In contrast, if you were in a position for 3-4 years, you should have some significant highlights and quantitative improvements you were able to achieve. Even in this case, 3-4 good solid bullet points should be sufficient. Save something to talk about during the interview. Bring out something that will WOW the interviewer. The resumé is to get you in the door, not to tell your whole life and work histories. For example, one of your bullet points could read:

- *Served as Reduction in Force & Succession Plan Project Manager resulting in 1.6 million dollar savings for the company in 6 months.*

The actual steps you took to accomplish this need not be spelled out on the resumé. Save that for the interview!

Q: What if I simply decide NOT to mention my military service or that I am in the Reserves?
A: Good question. What would it look like if you did not say that you served in the military? Well, it could be perceived by an employer that you are hiding something—that you are not being fully honest.

At the same time, there is a possibility that listing your military affiliation can cause a negative perception. For instance, with his employees serving in the reserves or deciding to do active duty to serve their country, an employer may wonder:

- *Will this service member deploy often?*
- *If the service member is deployed, am I going to have to train someone new and hire a backfill?*
- *How much time off will he/she need in order to attend additional military training throughout the year?*
- *The service member is extremely qualified, should I consider the person for promotion if they might soon leave?*

It's a challenge. What should you do? At some point in the interview process you may want to let your employer know you are in the Reserves. You want to be upfront, especially if you will be required to work on the weekends. This way the employer is not surprised when training comes up. You don't want to mislead or lie to the employer because that can become an ankle biter later.

The situation about your participation in the reserves may not be easy to discuss, but by being upfront, you maintain an open dialogue, and honesty is usually always appreciated and not usually punished. It is likely that if the potential employer is informed about the reserve commitment, he/she will be willing to work around it.

Q: Do I include my Reserve or military training on the resumé?
A: I think that is your personal choice for the resumé. However, you will want to include it on the application, as most applications will ask that question. Now, if the training you gained in the Reserves is relevant to the job, you may consider including it, and surely mention it during the interview.

Q: If I return to an employer after a deployment, is the employer obligated to give me back my old job?
A: The Uniformed Services Employment Reemployment Rights Act (USERRA) lists the responsibilities of both service members and employers in situations like this. The reality is, however, that many companies are coming up with devious ways to circumvent the requirements as outlined in the act, and there is a rise in cases of service members' rights being violated.

In one case I'm familiar with, a service member returned from a deployment to discover that five people who had less time and experience than he did had been promoted ahead of him. The service member approached the company in an attempt to find out his promotion status.

Now, in order to determine the service member's status in a case like this, you have to use something called the "escalator principle," which states that the employee will get back on the corporate "escalator" at the point he/she got off it when deployed and treated as if they did not leave. That sounds fair, but the escalator principle could also affect the service member negatively as well. For example, if the company had lay-offs while she was deployed, the service member could return to the escalator and lose her job when she returns since those layoffs would have affected her if she had been on the escalator with everyone else at that time.

It's really a tough situation to solve fairly for both sides.

Imagine you're an employer who hired a new employee several months to year ago to replace the service member who was deployed, and now that service member has returned in search of his/her old job. You think to yourself: *"I have this great employee I hired to replace Private Gomer Pyle, and now the company is making money! What am I going to do with the replacement employee? I have a small work force and really can't afford to (re)hire anyone. Doing that will cut into my profits."*

You can see the dilemma.

Companies are in business to make money, and being forced to maintain employees who may be absent due to deployments, and whose skill level and experience may be affected by their deployments, seems unfair. Meanwhile, the service member—who was temporarily "away on business" to protect the country—returns to a hostile job market where no loyalty exists either to his previous employment or his patriotic deployment.

Keep in mind, that there are many instances where a returning service member is, in fact, able to resume employment with no issues whatsoever. I, personally, had a positive experience when I joined the reserves some years ago. I notified my employer (the New York City Transit Authority), and they put me on "military leave" status while I completed basic training. While I was on leave, I was even considered for and *earned* two promotions. So, when I returned, I was placed back into my position in accordance with my seniority. This was pretty straightforward and easy because of the union rules and because promotions at the Transit Authority are seniority-based. So, when I returned, I was officially promoted, trained and placed in the proper seniority order as if I had not left for military duty.

But what do you do if your employer was not like mine? What if you know before you leave that your job will not be held open for you? What if you return from military service and your employer won't hire you back? (USERRA provides reemployment rights to you as a service member as long as you do not exceed five years of cumulative military service with each employer. Note: *Not all military orders count toward this 5-year time period.*)

Well, you could simply try to talk with your employer to negotiate an agreement to be rehired. If that does not work, you can seek assistance from Employer Support of the Guard and Reserve (ESGR) http://www.esgr.mil). An ESGR representative can educate the service member and employer with the terms of the Uniformed Services Employment Reemployment Rights Act (USERRA) in hopes the two parties can come to an agreement.

Keep in mind that ESGR representatives are volunteers and do not mediate cases. They simply offer guidance and information in order to help both parties reach agreement. Furthermore, they can devote only a limited time to your case before they recommend the case be closed. If the employer and employee cannot resolve their issue, then you, the service member, can decide whether to drop the case, seek private counsel or take it to the Department of Labor (DOL). In all honesty, the DOL is overworked and probably doesn't have the time or resources to properly address the load of cases they are receiving. It may not be worth the effort.

Here's something else to consider. How much time and energy do you want to devote to forcing an employer to hire you back if they really don't want to? Do you want to work in a job environment where you're not wanted? Let's say you get ESGR or DOL involved and you *do* get your job back because the employer is legally bound to hire you back and/or place you back in a particular position. What then? I can only imagine what an uncomfortable position you'd be in. You can bet that the company will look for opportunities to terminate you. That is why the law has been upgraded to provide the service member with one year of "protected" reemployment rights. However, the environment will likely be toxic.

For your information, the company can fire you because of:
1) Reduction in workforce
2) Sale or reorganization of the business
3) Stealing
4) Reoccurring lateness
5) Decline in business
6) Improper work habits

So if you feel that your employer is unjustly building a case to fire you for any of these reasons, then start to document conversations and interactions with your employer in the event you have to prove against their allegations.

I volunteer and serve as an ombudsman with the Department of Defense, Employer Support of the Guard and Reserve (ESGR) http://www.esgr.mil. The organization assists and educates service members and employers about USERRA. I can tell you that with the drawdown of Iraq and the closure of Afghanistan conflicts, I believe there is going to be a rise in more cases where service members' rights are violated under this act.

To learn more about both the employee's and employer's rights and obligations, visit the following link: http://www.esgr.mil/USERRA/USERRA-Links.aspx

The following website has a plethora of case studies of how service members have been affected to date by their military obligation. Take the time to read through and educate yourself on the different types of cases as this can affect your employment search. View it at: http://servicemembers-lawcenter.org

Q: Should I list my medals and honors? Do HR/hiring officials know what these medal/awards mean?
A: How relevant is your meritorious service medal, good conduct medal or global war on terrorism medal to the job at hand? If there is no connection between your medals/awards and the position you are interviewing for, then leave them off the resumé. You can talk about them the actual things you did to merit the recognition during the interview if the opportunity presents itself.

Q: Should I mention my secret or top-secret clearance when applying for a job?
A: In most cases, it's probably not necessary unless you're applying for a position that specifically requires you to have one. However, I suggest you talk briefly about it during the interview to show you were trusted with sensitive or classified information.

Q: What is the importance of highlighting my military service or multiple deployments in my professional summary?
A: Your summary should highlight your soft skills, people skills, organizational skills and project management skills etc. No matter what branch of service you served in, you had a specific job (i.e. mechanic, cook, intelligence, diver, infantryman, air traffic controller, transport, electrician, electronics technician, etc.).

This experience—more so than the specific branch of service—may qualify you for a position. Include that *experience* in the resumé and save anything else for the interview.

Should I carry resumés with me to a job fair?
You can to be prepared, but most companies are going to direct you to their website to upload and apply for positions. Your focus at the job fair is to make a connection with the person at the table

by using your well-polished 30-second "me commercial." Remember, you only have one time to make a first impression!

How important is it to have multiple degrees?
I am all in favor of higher education and think it is great, but theory without application and experience can hurt. Balance your education with some real life experience. Work part-time or volunteer to gain relevant experience.

Should I include "hours worked" on my resumé*?*
Not if you are applying for a civilian job, unless you believe it will add value to and increase your chances for interview and hire. I do not know of many jobs where you will work only 40 hours. What if the job you are applying for requires you to work overtime or what if you are on salary? Don't limit yourself.

However, if you are applying for a government position, the hours may be required [see the sample federal resumé in the Appendix.] So I recommend that you have at least two versions of your resumé.

I cannot address every possible scenario in this book or it will be hundreds of pages. I wrote this book to be direct, short and sweet, to the point so you can read it, get moving and WOPD...Oops! Did I just contradict myself with an acronym? WOPD = Work on Personally Developing!

Now, then, as you process all of that, let's take a little break and get to know a former service member and hear his story.

Chapter 7
Alfred: A Case Study

Alfred

I first met Alfred and his wife while *my* wife and I attended a marriage-networking event. We began to chat about our families and the type of work we did, and discovered we had a lot in common. We each had four children. We both served in the armed forces—me in the Army and he in the Navy—and we each had some background in human resources. Alfred had just recently graduated and received his Master's degree, while I, however, am still working towards my own Masters degree.

We talked a little about our experiences in the armed forces and how coincidental it was that, out of all the tables in the event, we should end up sitting together and having so much in common. We continued to converse and I let him know about my passion for helping people—particularly military service members and their families—navigate the interviewing and job hunt process. I told him and the other couples at the table about my experience with resumé writing and interviewing techniques. I gave everyone my business card and extended an offer to review their resumés and provide suggestions to help them improve. Alfred happened to be in between jobs and, as we said our goodbyes after the event, he said he'd be in touch. (By the way, in case you missed it, what Alfred and I were doing was plain and simple networking! Remember, it's either *network or NOT work!*)

A few weeks after the event, I received an email from Alfred in which he said, *"As per our discussion, here is a copy of my resumé. Let me know what you think, and if you have any leads, please let me know. FYI: I have applied to Walmart, Target,*

ABC company and DEF company for a Human Resources(HR) generalist position. So if you have any contacts please let me know. Thanks for your assistance!!"

I was glad that Alfred had followed through on my offer. I appreciated that his "cover letter" (the body of the email, in this case) indicated the position he was seeking. I viewed the resumé, and the first thing I noticed was that Alfred had squeezed a tremendous amount of information into it. As I mentioned earlier, giving too much information can sometimes work against the applicant, since the recruiter can't help but feel there's no reason to bring this person in for an interview when it appears they have listed everything they have ever done on the resumé.

I gave Alfred a call to discuss the resumé. I am tactful with my approach when coaching or giving feedback because I know that people often put a lot of time and effort in to putting a resumé together. I am careful about the way I provide the feedback because if people are anything like I was, they might go to the extreme making corrections based on other people's feedback all in search of that mythical "perfect" resumé.

"What kind of feedback have you received on your resumé so far?" I asked. I wanted to find out what advice others had given before jumping in with my own suggestions.

"Well, I've spoken with a few hiring officials and recruiters," he replied.

"Have you received any callbacks?"

"A few, not that many, and nothing panned out." The fact that he *did* receive a couple of telephone calls for interviews tells me the resumé was just "okay." Based on the tremendous amount of information he included in it, I knew that a recruiter had worked really hard to read it and pull out the information they were looking for, or simply that they were desperate to bring anyone in with even minimum experience to fill a position. Having met Alfred, I knew he was a good man, so the fact that he didn't receive many callbacks tells me the resumé could be improved to reflect more of his assets and value, and increase his callback ratio.

"What type of job are you looking for?" I asked further.

"Oh, I'm looking for anything! I need a job."

"I understand, but you have to be a bit more specific than that, especially with today's economy. Companies are not looking for someone to be the "Anything Manager," or "Team Leader of Whatever Needs to be Done," I joked. "They are looking for people who can solve their problems and operate safely. They are looking for experienced professionals who are coachable and can make an immediate impact solving problems, and helping the company save money and make money."

"Well, I'm definitely coachable, so I'm all ears!" he said.

A couple of the recommendations that I made included:

"Change the flow. It's hard to follow based on formatting and the dates worked at previous employers," I replied.

"Change the first sentence in your summary to start with the words 'highly qualified.' Also, there is no need to list MBA in professional summary as it will be listed under education."

"You have to tighten up your shot group and let people know what you are looking for in your 30-second 'Why you Should Hire Alfred' commercial or "elevator speech" as it's sometimes called. Imagine that you run into a company's top executive in the elevator of a building and only have 30 seconds—the length of time the elevator takes to get to the executive's top floor suite—to speak to him. What would you say in that thirty-second 'elevator speech' to sell him on hiring you or, at least getting a lead? While networking, you never know who you'll run into. So be prepared."

After our call, Alfred worked on the resumé based on my feedback. A few days later, I received another email from Alfred.

It read: *"Okay buddy, I took some of your advice, but I also changed some of the wording. Let me know what you think and how this one looks. Thanks for your assistance again. Just trying to get this thing in some order so I can start getting interviews, and hopefully lead to a career opportunity offer."*

Alfred's resumé was, in fact, getting better. I made a few more recommendations and sent it back to him. However, I didn't want him to spend too much time trying to create a perfect resumé, so I suggested that he start putting it out on the market to see what kind of response he would get. One way to judge how well your resumé is doing is to continue to use the first version as well as the improved version, and note which one scores the most callbacks.

Alfred did just that, and what do you know? He started getting callbacks and inquiries! That was an indication the resumé was improving, but we weren't finished yet. Now that he started to get called in for interviews, Alfred asked if I could take a look at some interview questions he thought would be good for him to ask.

"Take a look at my questions that I will ask the interviewer and let me know what you think," he asked me.

1-Do you see any gaps in my qualifications that I need to fill?
2-Are there any reasons I'm not fully qualified for this position?
3-Is there anything I've said that hurt my chances of being hired?
4-Now that you've had a chance to meet and interview me, what reservations would you have in putting me in this position?
5-What have I accidentally said or done during today's interview that's inconsistent with your perfect candidate for this job?

Alfred was definitely on the right track. He was being direct, humble, and was seeking constructive criticism from the interviewer. However, there were some flaws with how he phrased his questions. The first three are really "closed" questions that give the interviewer the option of simply saying "Yes" or "No" in response. Bad move. You want to ask open-ended questions to get the interviewer to give you more information than simply yes or no. You also do not want to draw attention to gaps in qualifications, or the things that you said throughout the interview. I offered Alfred my own list of suggested interviewee questions based on my philosophy that—like a seasoned salesperson—you want to be constantly 'closing' the deal throughout the interview.

"What qualifications not listed in the job description would you like the new hire to have?" This will give you an opportunity to understand what additional skills are required.

"What are your expectations of the new hire in the first 90 days on the job?" This gives you an understanding of what is expected of you and may be an opportunity to discuss additional training.

"How soon would you like me to start after I am selected for the position?" This is the assumptive close. You already see yourself in the position and express that confidently in this question.

"How many other people are being considered for this position?" It's not rude to ask this. You want to know who the competition is and where you fit in compared to others who are being considered.

"When will you make your final candidate selection to fill the job?" You want to get an idea when they will make the final selection so that if you are not called shortly thereafter, you can follow-up. Ask if that's okay.

Alfred took my advice, and after a few months of us working together, his interviewing activity increased, and that led to some job offers. Eventually, he found one that met his criteria and accepted it. However, it was not his dream job remembering what I told him—that the best time to look for work is while you are already working—he worked that first job for a short period of time and then found an even better opportunity about a month later! Even now, Alfred continuously updates his resumé and keeps it on the market in search of that next opportunity!

Feedback

Here is some feedback from others like Alfred who have been helped by the Rucksack to Briefcase process:

Q: What specific changes to your resumé were most helpful?
A: "You helped me to revamp the appearance of my resumé that opened the door(s) to receiving call backs, that lead to face-to-face interviews. You also helped me work through the logical layout and functional flow of my resumé."

Q: What advice did you recall that helped in the actual interview?
A: I found myself remembering you saying *"you want to always be closing the deal no matter if you like/want the opportunity or not!"*
A: You said *"always quantify your experience by putting it in terms of 'dollars saved,' 'redirection of funds', and/or 'future potential savings'—terms the employer values."*

Q: What would you advise others who are tweaking their resumés?
A: "Remember: the longer the length of time you were employed, the more bullet points you will have for that particular position."

Q: What do you know NOW, that you didn't know before?
A: Don't get comfortable. Always be on the hunt to better yourself and your financial situation. Keep acquiring new skills and experience to make yourself more marketable. Don't plant your feet. Leave room to uproot yourself for movement and growth!

Chapter 8
The Interview

So, you've created and tweaked your resumé. You've submitted it to various organizations and potential employers. You've notified your network of contacts that you are looking for employment. Hopefully, a few people have taken notice. They've reviewed your resumé and decided they want to learn more about you, so they pick up the phone, dial your contact number, and intend to invite you for an interview! This is what you've been waiting for! So, what do you do now???? First, don't screw it up!!

Callback Etiquette

Before we discuss interview strategies in depth, let's cover a little callback etiquette. Many people make it this far, and then totally screw things up by not knowing how to prepare for, answer or act during the actual callback! Here are a few tips to increase the probability of you *continuing* through the hiring process after receiving the call.

Be motivated, courteous and enthusiastic when you answer the phone. I can't tell you how many times I've called an applicant and felt that the very life energy was being sapped out of me!

Be ready! Saying to a recruiter *"Who is this?"* or *"What company are you with?"* because you've forgotten to which companies you applied is a no-no!! Wake-up! Stay alert! Be ready! Stay ready! *Note: keep a notepad by the phone or carry one with you indicating each company and the position you applied for.*

Do NOT—I repeat, (or say again over), do not say, *"I did not expect you to call so soon."* You will earn yourself a spot at the bottom of a large pile of resumés.

Do not say *"Can I call you back?"* Typically, a recruiter or hiring manager will ask if this is a good time to speak for about 20-30 minutes or however long they need. If you happen to be driving, or in the middle of something, this is your time to put your sales skills to use. You can say something like, *"WOW, I am excited that you called! However, I am driving is there a time later today we can speak?"* Let them answer. Then you can tell them, *"I will be available in the next 30 minutes/ 2 hours/tomorrow around 2pm. Would it be possible to talk then?"* Let them answer. Then, before you hang up the phone, make sure you're sure who is supposed to call whom, get the caller's name, a contact number and an email address if possible. Thank them for the opportunity to talk about the position they are hiring for.

Note: If the time they suggest is really not a good time, do not be afraid to say so. As a recruiter, I would rather you reschedule than to conduct a call with background music, children crying, or while you're eating or driving.

Once, when I was searching for a job, there was a persistent recruiter from a search firm who was hounding me to schedule a telephone interview with a company he had found for me. He first made contact with me while I was deployed and I told him it was not a good time to setup a telephone interview. I should have followed my instincts and delayed the call until I was truly in position to present my best. However, he pushed and pushed and claimed to have talked to the company and said they still wanted to speak with me regardless.

Well, I allowed myself to be convinced to conduct the telephone interview. I conducted the interview and, because I was on deployment and not in the right mental frame of mind, I do not think I did my best. Sure enough, after the interview, I contacted the recruiter to get the company feedback. He never returned my call. I'm convinced it was because I didn't present myself well during that phone interview. That experience taught me a valuable lesson: the search firm recruiters work for the companies they represent and not you the potential employee. His actions and character led me to sever the relationship, and resolve never to allow myself to be forced to conduct an interview before I'm ready.

The Interview

Now then, I'm going to let you in on a secret. If a recruiter calls you for an interview, it means they've read your resumé and already determined you have some of the skills to do the job. The purpose of the interview is to get to know you *and* to determine if you are a good fit for the culture. These days, companies are looking closely to see if you fit in with the culture of the department, team or organization to which you'll be assigned. Here is the opportunity for you to demonstrate to the person conducting the interview that you are, in fact, the right fit, *and* that you have the skills to do the job, too!

Hopefully you have prepared yourself for the interview by doing some research about the company and learning a little about the existing culture. As an interviewer, one of the first questions I ask after the standard *"Tell me a little about yourself?"* is *"How much do you know about company ABC?"*

Interview types

You have only one time to make a first impression and you want to make it count. My best advice to you is to act from the mindset that *anytime* you come in contact with someone from the company consider that you are *still* in the interview process, especially if you do not have an offer. Don't let your guard down or lower your standards. Always act professionally and demonstrate excellence at all stages of the interview process, even if you think you may not want to work at the company. You never know how a good first and follow-through impression can benefit you. Someone in the hiring process may say to you, *"Look, you are not a good fit for our organization but I have a friend who is looking for someone with your skills,"* and may just refer you.

I want to get you in the right mind frame when you approach an interview. Think for a moment to your time in the military. What were your actions or the actions of your squad, platoon or flight prior to going on a mission. Think of an interview as a mission. Your mission is to arrive on time, know the location of the building, know who you will be interviewing with, and know something about the company. With Google and the Internet as ever-present resources, it is "mission failure" if you are not prepared.

Prior to going on a mission in your perspective branch of service you received intel about the area you were going into information about the "friendlies" and "combatants" (in this case it would be the company you are interested in and competitors). Do not forget to do your pre-interview check—a concept similar to your pre combat checks in the military.

1) Make sure you have extra copies of your resumé
2) Something to write with

3) Make sure you are in the correct uniform (suit, tie, dress, pant suit) and dress appropriately for the interview
4) Know where to park-this will be provided by hiring officials
5) Give yourself ample time to arrive early so that even if there's a major accident or a flat tire, you can still arrive on time. Tardiness is inexcusable. Think about your military service. What were the consequences if you did not make movement? Have a primary and alternate plans of action. You have it in you. This is the time to demonstrate the great training you received during your service.

An interview run through

Here are ten questions an interviewer may ask a prospective employee. They include some standard questions as well as some "curve balls" the interviewer may throw at you that you should be prepared for.

1) *Tell me a little about yourself.* This can be tricky and you want to stay in the guidelines of the elevator speech (i.e. where you are from, background, your interest.) Or what I usually say is, " Wow I've done a lot! What would like to know specifically?"

2) *What do you know about our company ABC?* You had better have done some research or this will guarantee you an exit from the interview—real quick!

3) *Why do you want to work for company ABC?*
Don't say "Just for the money, really!" Mention how it might further the growth of the overall industry, enhance your career, give you an opportunity to make a contribution based on some ideas you have or be a productive member of society!

4) *Could you tell me about a time where you had a challenge convincing your manager/supervisor about a particular procedure? What was the outcome?*
This is a "behavioral" question that seeks to determine how you handle conflict, authority, and your conviction to your ideas.

5) *What is your current salary?* They ask this to find out where you are and what they could offer you and make it a good deal!

6) *Could you tell me about a time where you were given a task without complete details.* This is an opened ended question and the interviewer will not ask what happened, or what was the result. This is a time where you can knock the ball out of the park!

7) *What is your salary expectation?*
My advice is to prolong or delay the salary question if you can. The way you answer the question can perhaps cost you to not be offered the job especially if you are too high in range. So it is important to know what the market is paying and you can look at other sites like glass door, indeed, salary.com and in some cases you can do a Google search of the position at the company to see if a previous employee have posted salary/salary range. You can also connect with recruiters who can help you with a market/salary analysis. You have several options for how to respond:

1) *"What do you have budgeted for the position?"* (It is fair game to ask this question)

2) *"Are you offering me the position? Make me an offer and we can go from there!"*

3) *"Are you asking me what I would like to earn?"*

4) Give them a wide/vague range of where you are or where you want to be

5) Refuse to reply on the grounds of confidentiality

6) Provide total compensation information without specifying the salary component. In other words, provide salary including bonus without specifying either specifically.

7) Put dashes on application to show that you saw the question but decline to comply or provide either actual or false salary figures.

8) Or you can be direct and ask for the salary that you want.

Some applicant tracking systems will not allow you to advance through the applications without placing a number in the box. So you can put a desired salary in the box or in some cases I have placed 0.00's in the box. That's a chance that I took by not listing an actual number.

I have heard some employers will ask for proof of salary such as a W2 and some will do so in the background investigation but I believe this is invasion of privacy. They could easily figure out typical salary numbers by looking at industry surveys or other online resources. I have yet to have that happen to me personally.

If you are trying to make a significant jump in salary then the time to do so is when you are changing jobs or careers.

1) You have to convince them why you are worth what you are seeking and be sure to quantify that number.

2) You can tell them what you are currently earning: *"I am currently making 50k, and my present employer would agree I am worth more, but with budget constraints, salary freeze, challenges in the industry, I'm stuck, even though the standard for someone with my skills and years of experience is 80k. That is one of the reasons that I am transitioning or moving on."*

3) You can also say that I am making in the mid……80's, low 70k….the high 60k which includes a 5%, 10% Basic Additional Allowance and a comprehensive benefits package.

Then transition immediately into the question: *"What is the compensation range for THIS position?"* This transitional question allows you flexibility and attempt to get the employer to provide you some compensation data.

Is it a good idea to answer the expected salary question directly?

It is not necessarily a good idea to answer the interviewer directly initially. You can redirect the question by asking them what they have budgeted for the position. You can give a salary range and ask them directly what the salary range for the position that you are interviewing for? Once again it is a two way street and a mutual conversation just as they want your current salary, you want to know what they are offering as well. The company should be willing to provide the salary range they are offering for the position.

Is it normal for an interviewer to ask this?

This is a normal question an interviewer will ask you early on in the interview process, so you need to practice how you are going to respond. The follow-up question is *"what is your salary expectation?* This is where doing your homework comes into play about what the market is paying. You can defer the question by saying: *"I need to know more about the position, my scope of duties and responsibilities, would it be okay to discuss salary later in the process?"* Or you can say that you expect to be offered a salary equivalent to the industry standard

If you *do* give a salary range ask, the following question: *"How close am I within the salary range that you have budgeted for the position?"* or *"Is that within the ball park of what you have budgeted for the position?"*

Another option is to simply not answer the question.

If I do answer, won't I shoot myself in the foot if my current salary is currently low?

You will most certainly shoot yourself in the foot if your salary is low and especially lower than what they are paying for the position. You have to find a way and convince them why you are the one for the position. Be confident about what you bring to the table and communicate that they will miss the benefit of having you a part of the team.

1) Talk about how you improved processes at your current and previous jobs
2) How you helped save the previous companies money with correlate to helping them make money
3) How you operate safe and how well of a good steward you are over budgets and finance

There are arguments both for and against each of the strategies of providing information upfront, accurate, but candidates often wonder if employers will be able to verify any past salary information they supply. The complex answer is they may be able to verify. Typically previous employers wont give out that information. They verify that you worked at the company, position and the time period you were employed.

The simple advice: practice, practice, practice. Do not put all your eggs in one basket ie... applying for one job at one company the probability that you will land with this high percentage is tough. Know what you bring to the table, and

Be Confident in your skills, desperation will cost you leverage and will be written all over your face!

Be Convincing in your interview and message!

Be Competitive in your salary negotiations!

Be prepared to negotiate. Companies expect you to do so, but do so **_ONLY_** after a formal offer has been made.

You can also be frank and let the interviewer know what it will take for you to make a move. If you get to the point of the offer you have some leverage because they have invested time in you and like you, what skills you bring to the table and they are willing to negotiate

Closing the Deal and Evaluating the Offer

Now that you have wowed the potential employer in the interview, your next goal is to get an offer. Stay enthusiastic and continue to express your excitement for the job. Let them know you are interested! You may want to ask:

How many people are currently being considered for the position?
Will you be interviewing anyone else for the position?
When will you make the final decision and select a candidate?

If they tell you they "will call you," or that they'll "know something by a specific day," understand that they are busy and may not get around to getting back to you. Therefore, ask the interviewer if it would be okay to follow-up with them after a specific date. Typically, they will say yes. (The squeaky wheel gets the oil.) I recommend sending a thank you card. It is more personable (and rare) to send a handwritten thank you card rather than an email. My advice is to do whatever will set you apart from all the other people who have interviewed for the position.

Now then. It is not usually a good idea to accept an offer on the spot. At that moment of success, you are at your most emotional state and may not make the best decision. Postpone your decision for at least a day or two to gain a little perspective and time to evaluate the entire offer.

To evaluate an offer, you'll need to know how it compares to your current military salary, *plus* the dollar value of your Basic Additional Housing (BAH), Basic Additional Subsistence (BAS) allowance, uniform allowance and any other additional entitlements. You'll need to do some salary research to know what the reasonable going rates are. Also, compare any bonuses, and medical benefits the company is offering to determine if it is, in fact, a good deal for you and your family.

How to Decline an Offer

Before *declining* an offer, I hope you've negotiated and determined that (a) the offer does not meet your expectations, or (b) you've accepted or are considering another offer.

1) The first step is to acknowledge receipt of the formal offer and thank those involved in the process. I recommend you do so by email and telephone not by sending a text.

2) Find out how and when they would like you to respond to the offer. If there is another potential offer on the table, you can let them know you are considering it. Remain professional and do not pit one party against the other in order to get a better offer.

3) While you are going through the decision-making process, stay in contact via email or through telephone conversations with the potential employer

4) If you do not accept the offer, inform the employer, recruiter or any other intermediary know your decision by phone. This shows courtesy to everyone. They may be disappointed, but I am sure they will respect your decision.

If you decline the offer appropriately (with courtesy, honesty and respect for everyone's valuable time), that can leave a positive perception in the minds of the recruiter and hiring officials. They may even reach out to you for future assignments.

The reality of anti-military discrimination

Discrimination is a fact of life in our society. Under the law, you are entitled to fair and equitable employment regardless of where you fall in any of the "protected classes" of potential discrimination (gender, race, skin color, age, religion and sexual orientation). Personally, I think being in the military should also be a "protected class" since it can hurt you if it's on your resumé.

It can be difficult to prove, but if you've completed your 2nd, 3rd or final interview or even been given a job offer, and then, after bringing up your affiliation with the reserves, that offer was rescinded, that could be a possible violation of the law.

First check with the Employer Support of the Guard and Reserves (ESGR) a Department of Defense organization at http://www.esgr.mil/USERRA/USERRA-Contact.aspx or 1-800-336-4590 (select option 1) between 8 AM and 6 PM EST where they can determine if you have a valid USERRA claim.

If valid, the ESGR has ombudsmen who mediate between you and your employer to remedy the situation. The remedy is an action that will bring the employer into compliance with the law.

This is a good option because it helps the service member maintain a working relationship with the employer.

If your employer is uncooperative, the other route is to file a formal complaint with the Department of Labor (DOL), or hire a lawyer who specializes in USERRA, employment cases.

If the DOL is unable to resolve the case, it can be escalated to Attorney General (for private/state employees) or to the Office of Special Counsel. Government lawyers can enforce the USERRA laws but only take a few of the many cases that are filed.

USERRA cases can drag on for long periods of time. As mentioned earlier, you must decide if it's a worthwhile investment of your time, or if it's wiser to simply move on.

Chapter 9
Michelle: a Case Study

Michelle

During my deployment to Kuwait in 2011-2012, there was a large population of service members in the area who were returning home to unemployment and under-employment. There was one particular group from the National Guard in Minnesota where fully 20% of the three thousand soldiers returning home would *not* have jobs waiting for them. Finding jobs for those service members was an important challenge.

To help with the transition back to civilian work life I arranged and conducted interviewing and resumé classes in Kuwait entitled "Recruiting & Resumé 101." The class was open to anyone who wanted to attend--service members, active duty, reserves, retirees and even contractors. I emailed a flyer to see if there was some interest. Little did I know just how much interest there was actually going to be!

Fifteen people showed up to that first meeting. There was a large response from service members from all the branches—Navy, Air Force, Army National guard and reserve. There were service members who attended my classes from around the country—all 50 states! There were a few active duty service members—primarily those who were considering transitioning or retirement or for basic knowledge because active duty was their fulltime job. In the next meeting, an officer on base set up a class for 30 people from his unit alone.

Many attendees admitted they volunteered for deployment just to have an income. They were willing to serve and, in most cases, put themselves in harm's way just to have income coming in to meet their financial obligations—even at the expense of being separated from loved ones. Several other service members were trying to extend their deployment because the prospect of returning home to unemployment was becoming a frightening reality.

I remember helping one particular soldier from the National Guard whom I'll call "Michelle." Michelle, an educated soldier, was divorced with three children and was returning home to unemployment. The unemployment rate for her state for veterans was more than three times the state's civilian unemployment rate of 5.7 percent.

Michelle was excited about the class I was presenting and even searched around the base for others to attend. I gave a survey to get feedback from the students to make sure I was presenting relevant material because I wanted them to walk away with some new information and even experience an "Aha!" moment.

Participants who attended included those from pay grades E-1 through O-6, a full bird colonel, a senior commissioned officer who was with the Air Force Reserve, as well as a Lieutenant Colonel Chaplain. Most importantly, they wanted to know how to create an effective resumé, how to interview, and how to uncover the value of their military experience that is often lost in translation when conveying it in language that a layperson will understand.

Michelle attended the first of several classes that I put on in Kuwait in 2012. She later gathered a class of about 25 attendees for me to present as a two-day 4-hour session. I was caught off guard when I opened the conference room door, but excited at the same time to know there were so many people in our immediate surrounding area who needed assistance and whom I could help.

Michelle asked if I would review her resumé because she had a few jobs in the states for which she wanted to apply. I reviewed her resumé at the beginning, but held off providing immediate feedback. First, I didn't want to de-motivate her with too much constructive criticism, and second, I wanted her to apply the information she learned in class and make changes herself as necessary. In this case, I believe Michelle understood the information and began to edit the resumé on her own and gave me a revised version soon after the first. As the process continued, with my guidance and my recommendations, it slowly became a quality product to start putting into market place.

Several weeks after the class, when the resumé was just about where it needed to be, she informed me that she saw a job that she was interested in applying for. She applied for that and other jobs and also attended a virtual job fair. Soon afterwards, she received an email from one company that wanted to conduct a telephone interview.

I gave her some pointers on how to handle the phone interview, and afterwards, we talked about it. She believed it went well and that my class had given her the confidence to ask specific questions. The class taught her to treat the interview as a conversation and to speak confidently as "partner" rather than simply an "employee" seeking a job. I taught her to view the employer as simply someone with a problem who is trying to find someone to fix that problem. The mission is to exchange your talent, skills and abilities and to agree upon a compensation package for the exchanging of those skills. It is a little less stressful when you take the partnership approach/mindset.

Michelle had a second interview conducted via Skype®. That one was a little uncomfortable, but went pretty well. Michelle was still in Kuwait, but she understood the value of submitting her resumé and doing this work *in advance* of her return to the states.

We lost touch for a few months, and then I ran into her while we were both attending a military course in Kuwait. She expressed excitedly how she eventually landed a job with a good company back home and thanked me for my assistance. She continues to expand her network and keeps her mind open for any opportunity that may come her way. She said, "Chief Ray, I remembered something you said during your class that stuck with me, '*the best time to look for work is when you have work!*'"

Chapter 10
Beyond Deployment & Employment

Entrepreneur, as defined by the Merriam-Webster dictionary, is *a person who starts a business and is willing to accept the risk of loss in order to make money.*

The Census bureau reported that veteran owned businesses numbered more than 2 million in 2007, and hundreds of thousands of service disabled veteran business owners accounted for 9% of all businesses nationwide. They generated trillions of dollars of revenue, so that tells you and me there is opportunity out there to be business owners if we choose. Veteran owned businesses contribute and add great value to the economy. Contribution to the country is nothing new for you because you have sacrificed and contributed during your service time.

I want to use this final chapter, therefore, to talk to you about using your gifts, talents and abilities to work for yourself. Yes I said it! Become an entrepreneur business owner because you have been leading your organization and in some cases running a business within your respective unit in the military!

As we know, whether you have served short term or long term in the military, the transition back to civilian life and work can be a challenging and difficult. You may find after landing your first job that you simply do not enjoy the work that is available; can't fit into the environment and culture. You can turn your transition, ordinary working life to becoming an entrepreneur.

Risk, she says!

The dictionary offers a key requirement of entrepreneurship: the willingness to take risks. Are you kidding me? You, my friend, understand risk. Yes, you "worked" for someone else, but you opened yourself up to risk from the day you signed up and took the oath of enlistment to defend the constitution at the potential cost of loss of life. You have risked during the course of service as well as across the battlefield. But again you worked for someone else.

You know more than you know

Now, being an entrepreneur is not for everyone. However, I will throw out some ideas of what you've already doing and suggest how it might transition nicely into a business venture no matter what branch of the military you gained the experience.

If you were a *cook*, you've learned how to prepare meals for hundreds or even thousands of people several times a day, for several years. You could transition nicely into owning your own catering service or teaching others how to do it!

How about a *transport operator*? You drove hundreds of miles safely over dangerous highways conducting convoys, delivering supplies, equipment and fuel. You might transition nicely into an owner/operator trucking company delivering the same things you did in the military.

Whether you were a trainer, public speaker, personnel administration specialist, mechanic, heavy-duty equipment operator, infantryman, military police officer, electrician, or electronic technician, there are skills you now possess which offer the expertise to own and operate your own business.

Of course, you do not have to go into business doing what did in the military. As ex-military, you are also a manager, a leader and a visionary, so as a business owner you can *hire* people who are experts to generate money for your business.

I used to work as a civil servant in New York City for one of the better organizations with great benefits. I did that for eight years and held four different positions as a result of promotions and advancement. I had what others would consider a "good job." However, I didn't like the thought of having to do 30 years of service in order to earn a retirement at half my working salary. I knew I had to do something.

Someone shared a network marketing business opportunity with me in the telecommunications industry that just made sense. I took a chance and started working as an independent representative (my own business) on a part-time basis, and over time I developed an organization that extended across the country and that served thousands of customers and generated me a monthly salary gave me the courage to walk away from that "good job."

I had been contemplating leaving my job for while, but the straw that really pushed me to take the plunge was when I needed a couple of days off and I was told "you are number 10 on this day and 15 on this day." In other words, there were either 10 or 15 people *ahead* of me who had requested time off. That was enough for me to ask, "How do I resign from this position?"

And that's exactly what I did! It was a bit scary at the time, but simply taking the leap and having thoughts of independence and freedom in my head miraculously attracted the opportunities and the people I needed to assist me. Most rewarding, however, was that this experience helped me to grow and develop to be the person I am today.

The business acumen I gathered has helped me be more successful at everything I do. Even when, I worked for the Army as a recruiter, I treated it as my own business. My job was to sell the Army and recruit qualified men and women into the Army. In my mind, however, I was getting new customers and building relationships with stakeholders.

The military gave me all the tools necessary to be successful: a vehicle, a cell phone, an office, metrics to measure success and failure, a sense of competition, plus awards and recognition. As a result, I learned and perfected my people skills, as well as sales and marketing skills.

You plan, strategize and implement. You are decisive. You have worked at all levels and roles with various responsibilities. You have the entrepreneur spirit where you operate independently in the best interest of your organization, you are disciplined, self starting. You produce reports, lead teams of service members, are accountable for people and high dollar value equipment. You meet and exceed metrics. You understand "profit and loss" in stark, real human terms, and you understand "competitive advantage" in ways others never will.

Lets face it, there are thousands of individuals coming off active duty at this time. When you combine that reality with the unemployment rates, starting your own business should be considered as one option.

I won't get into all the details here (perhaps *a Combat to CEO* book is in order), but business ownership can take the form of, require or involve:

Part-time	Small investment	Passive income
Full-time	Large investment	Residual income
From home	For Profit	Passive income
Storefront	Not for profit	
Franchise		

The way you structure your business, who you serve, how/where you operate, and what form of income is generated are all under your control.

Resources

There are many resources available for you as a service member to start a business. The Small Business Association (SBA) has tons of information on starting a business. The SBA provides free, individual, face-to-face as well as Internet counseling for small businesses, and low-cost training to first-time entrepreneurs and established small businesses. To make use of these services, contact one of the SBA's offices and ask about their Small Business Development Centers.
http://www.sba.gov/content/veteran-service-disabled-veteran-owned

You can get information and support on writing a business plan to finance and grow the business. There are opportunities for veterans who want to purchase a franchise and you can find that information by visiting the Veteran's Administration veterans' page and click on business:
http://www.va.gov/

Why now?

Right now it is easier than ever to start a business. You have more resources available than entrepreneurs of old:
    Access to tons of information
    Access to capital in the form of grants
    Access to different technology (internet)
    Access to global markets
    Less risk and high potential Return on Investment (ROI)

Note: Going into business for themselves—particularly Internet-based—may be the ideal solution for military spouses/family members who find themselves moving every 2-3 years, and trying to find work with a track record that shows every new employer you'll probably be there just a while. Perhaps it's time to start and run a part/full-time business from home!

So if working for someone is not for you, take the initiative, step outside of conformity and go for it! There are many before you and many behind you who will go down that business ownership route. The only one that will stop *you* from doing the same is you. Look doubt and fear in the eye and take the hill!

Business ownership is not for everyone. However, the military is reducing forces and reducing costs. There will not be enough jobs for the amount of people who will be transitioning. Don't be left behind.

Passion

One of the best first steps before starting any venture is the same as if you were seeking employment. Remember I suggested you take the time to decide what field you enjoy? Well, a business based on your hobbies, interests and natural talents will be the best combination of practicality and passion. Towards that end, I suggest you do what I did and turn your passion into profit. My mentor for this book, Walt Goodridge, is the man who coined the term "passionpreneur," and is author of *Turn Your Passion Into Profit*. He's a master at helping people discover their purpose, harness their passion, create products and market them for profit. You can find him online at http://www.passionprofit.com! Tell him Chief Raymond sent you!

A Rucksack to Briefcase Master Checklist

Here are few *Rucksack to Briefcase* steps you can take right now, ...even if you are still on active duty.

Research (Goal: gain clarity about your goals)
☐ Determine what industry, position, salary and culture you want
☐ Write down what your ideal job and ideal day would be
☐ Find and speak with others who have been successful

Networking Preparation (start to build a network)
☐ Set up a LinkedIn® account and start connecting
☐ Set a goal to have 100 connections in the first 30 days
☐ Create Youtube® interview video
☐ Modify your email signature
☐ Create logbook: company name, position applied and contact
☐ Join networking groups and organizations
☐ Set a goal to meet new people each day, week and month
☐ Let people know you are looking for work and ask for leads

Resumé Preparation
☐ Create first draft of resumé
☐ Create 3 versions of resumé (At least a government version)
☐ Have 3 people whom you respect critique and provide feedback
☐ Begin applying for jobs you see online

Interview Preparation
☐ Practice your 30-second "me commercial" so it is crisp
☐ Practice mock interviews with friend or advisor
☐ Clean up your online image
☐ Research the companies you have applied to

A Final Word from Chief Raymond

I truly believe that, as a result of your military training, you are the best-trained talent available. However, it will be up to you to look yourself in the mirror, believe it for yourself and communicate that effectively as you move from Rucksack to Briefcase!

I hope this book has helped you in some small way. I invite you to visit the Civilianside.com website for more information, updates and any other helpful links and information I find that can help you go from rucksack to briefcase! Exelsior!

—**Chief Raymond**

Chief Warrant Officer Raymond is available for
Speaking engagements
Resumé assistance, and
One-on-one coaching sessions
For more information:
email chiefray@civilianside.com
sign up at www.civilianside.com

Appendix
Resources

What the Military Will Never Tell You

I want to touch on three ideas that I think I are important to anyone making a transition from deployment, active duty, combat and a life in the military.

1. What you do for a living

It is not natural to kill people for a living.

We live in an aberrant society. Despite what you've been led to believe, despite the long history of us as human beings doing so, killing other human beings is not a normal thing. It has consequences. Warfare is not natural. It is not natural to live for hours, days, months and years under the threat of death. It is not natural to be fired upon day after day as a target, nor to do so to others. It is not natural to see people dismembered and killed. Such experiences have consequences.

No, it is not natural. Anyone who attempts to convince you otherwise has either never seen active duty, or is being paid to recruit you. The experience of killing other humans detaches you from reality. It forces you to construct a new reality and belief system in order to justify the killings.

The challenges that service members face integrating into civilian side society (with its own aberrations best left for another book), the challenges finding a job

2. "Others return from war and appear to be holding it together"

I will say two things:

(a) Appearances are deceiving. You'll never really know what is going on inside the mind of an individual who appears to be "holding it together." You may never know what it is like to

actually live daily with such an individual. Because admitting that there are real psychological, emotional and physiological effects to a life of killing has already been made taboo as an act of weakness. Such an individual may take that belief system and the façade they are living with them to their graves.

(b) It doesn't matter. It doesn't matter if someone else appears to be holding it together. You are a different human being. There is no standard coping procedure when it comes to dealing with emotional trauma. The outward appearance of others coping does not negate the reality of what *you* are going through. It does not mean that PTSD (Post-Traumatic Stress Disorder) is not real.

Yes, there are consequences and effects of experiencing war. The mantra of "just following orders" will neither absolve nor cure you of the effects of the trauma you have endured. For cure to occur, there must be a day of reckoning. By that I mean you must take personal accountability for what you have done even if it runs counter to the standard paradigm of your gender identity, of your military identity, or of our identity as a nation.

Here is a simple exercise of accountability:

On a piece of paper, describe in as much detail as possible the instances of violence, destruction and murder you may have committed. Write down the date, time, place, people involved and the exact sequence of events exactly as they occurred. Write what you know you did. Write what the consequences were. You never have to share this with anyone, but the simple act of admission, of acceptance and accountability can relieve a tremendous pressure from your mind, heart and soul.

3. Your Health and Well Being

During active duty abroad, you were exposed to chemicals and environments that have changed you. You know this to be true. You smelled it. You tasted it. You felt it. You feel it even now. You do not need anyone to justify, validate or confirm something you know to be true. These chemicals have effects. The challenges you face making and keeping relationships; the challenges you face finding and keeping a job; the challenges simply concentrating long enough on an application, and challenges you face in all aspects of your homeland deployment could all be affected by the chemical changes in the balance of your body, blood and brain.

You are not being delusional about these effects. You remember who you were before deployment, and you know who you are now. Something changed. Anyone who attempts to convince you otherwise has never been in combat, or if they have, they have a vested interested in limiting the military's perceived legal liability for your care.

Now, you can fight for your right to receive this care if that is your calling. However, regardless of how such a fight resolves itself in the courts, it is still incumbent upon you—and you alone—to seek and find treatments for your condition. The good news is, such treatments exist. They may not be covered by your benefits, but they exist.

Chelation therapy. Herbal Detox. Hot Yoga. Clay therapy. Sauna detoxification. Hydrotherapy and more are all ways to remove toxic substances (alcohol, drugs, years of prescriptions) from the body. Start seeking.

My simple point is that you might be surprised how (1) acknowledgement of the aberrance of it all, (2) a subtle shift in guilt and the acceptance of truth, and (3) of flushing toxins out of your system; all may improve your ability to adopt the right attitude, re-integrate more effectively in your homeland deployment, find and keep the job you are seeking, and make the ultimate best transition from rucksack to briefcase.

--Anonymous

Chief Raymond's Homeland Deployment Survey for Service Members

While writing this book, I surveyed many individuals to get their input to make the book as helpful as possible. Here are some of the questions I asked in that survey, along with just a few of the many great and insightful responses. –Chief Raymond

What is the most challenging part of deployment?
"Not being there for my family, and experiencing the loss of friends / members of my military in war zones."
Jeff R. (Male/Married/Army/National Guard- Reserves/O1-O5/served 1-4 years/deployed 3-5 times/Iraq, State Side)

How has military service changed you?
"I feel disconnected from home. I have found that in the civilian population politics run work. I do not operate that way. My military training has paid off in dedication to the job."
--**Teresa T.** (Female / Divorced / Army / National Guard Reserves / O6-O10 / served 26-30+ years / deployed 5+ times/Iraq)

"In the beginning, the first year after I returned from Afghanistan, I felt completely alone. As if no one understood. It caused a lot of hurt and resentment. I have also found that I am much more emotional about things. But I have worked things out very well with my loved ones especially my husband because of his patience and understanding."
--**Terry** (Female / Married / Army / National Guard-Reserves /E5-E9 / served 21-25 years / deployed 1-2 times / Afghanistan, State Side)

"My experience has changed me in numerous ways. I truly understand and embrace the key tenets of leadership and service, I can maintain my commitment level even in ambiguous and austere environments, my awareness level of my surroundings has increased, I feel that soldiers possess a lot of special training and expertise and if positioned and committed to these assets could add value to any organization."
--**Jeff** (Male / Married/Army/National Guard-Army Reserves/ O1-O5/ served 1-4 years / Deployed 3-5 times / Iraq, State Side)

"I have been schooled in the skill of flexibility and quickly adapting to change. I have learned how to effectively work with members of diverse groups!" --**Elizabeth** (Married/Spouse)

What is the most significant and noticeable change OTHERS have commented on you about since you've been back?

"As the military is the enforcement arm of foreign policy, you gain a greater appreciation for foreign policy. The one thing that stands out is how having gone to the middle east, my comments on middle eastern policy have much more weight." --**Bryan** (Male/Married/Army/Active Duty/AGR/O1- O5/served 5-10 years/deployed 1-2 times/Iraq)

"My husband stated that I have become too emotional. My best friend says I show too little emotion." --**Terry** (Female / Married / Army / National Guard- Reserves / E5-E9/ served 21-25 years / deployed 1-2 times / Afghanistan)

"More focused and serious about my life currently and in the future."--**Jeff R**. (Male / Married / Army / National Guard-Reserves/O1- O5/served 1-4 years/deployed 3-5 times/Iraq)

How has military life changed your family interaction?

"My family life has changed somewhat due to my deployment / mobilizations and my inability to attend several key events but I try to keep all my family members in the loop and aware. We try to incorporate new tools to stay connected no matter where I am."
--**Jeff R.** (Male/Married/Army/Reserves/O1- O5/served 1-4 years/deployed 3-5 times/Iraq, States)

"I learned I wasn't the only one to deploy. Meaning, although my family did not physically deploy, they still had to make adjustments back home. The reconnection was a process we both had to go through." --**Bryan** (Male/Married/Army/Active Duty/AGR/O1-O5/served 5-10 years/deployed 1-2 times/Iraq)

What are some ways military experience has made you exceptionally qualified for a regular civilian job?

"My three positions on Active Duty were, Planning Officer, Security Manager, and Civil Engineer. Planning, attention to detail, security, and Engineering are all relevant skills I picked up in the military." --**Bryan** (Male/Married/Army/Active Duty/AGR/O1- O5/served 5-10 years/deployed 1-2 times/Iraq)

"It made me a better time manager. It allowed me to sharpen my inter-personal skills. Made me realize that you have to get people engaged and believing in your mission and task in order to get them done. You have to make sure that you have "buy in" from your subordinates/team members. Therefore, I have made sure that I make the connection with my subordinates and peers in order to accomplish the goals I have set for my staff and myself."
--**Dwyanne** (Male / Single / Army / National Guard/Army Reserves/ E5-E9 / served 21-25 years / 92A408 / deployed 3-5 times / Iraq, Stateside)

"I attended scores of electrical and electronic schools in the Navy. The Navy also allowed me to study, troubleshoot, and perform maintenance on various complex electronic and computer suites. The Navy also allowed me to attend college and earn my degree with a specialty in electro-mechanics."
--**R Gomez** (Male/Married/Navy/DOD Civilian/Contractor/O1-O5/served 11-16 years/deployed 5+ times/Iraq, Other)

How is your service in the military viewed by your employer?
"They say they are military friendly but the last time I informed them of going on orders they took me from full time to part time 2 days later." –**SunShine** (Female/Single/Army/Active Duty/ AGR / O1- O5 / served 21-25 years / deployed 1-2 times/Iraq)

"Looked upon as a positive. The employers I have been with value my work ethic and military experience. I've found that discipline, professionalism, and honor are always looked upon by potential employers as a good thing." --**Dwyanne** (Male / Single / Army/National Guard / Army Reserves / E5- E9 / served 21-25 years / 92A408 / deployed 3-5 times / Iraq, stateside)

Do you believe your military service has helped or hurt your chances of promotion?
"It has helped because I am able to continually practice and also try things during a drill that I may not have the latitude to perform during normal business setting, then perform an evaluation of how it went and then put it into a civilian environment." --**Dwyanne** (Male / Single / Army/National Guard / Army Reserves / E5- E9 / served 21-25 years / 92A408 / deployed 3-5 times / Iraq, stateside)

"Used to believe it helped but after recent events with employer I would say it hurt." --**SunShine** (Female/Single/Army/Active Duty/AGR/O1- O5/served 21-25 years/deployed 1-2 times/Iraq)

What things do you have to constantly remind yourself in order to make the transition smoother?
*"Stay focused on the positive aspects
What's for me, I will get...
Life is not about the tasks, but its about the journey and all experiences are and can be learning experiences."* –**Jeff** (Married/Army/National Guard-Army Reserves/O1- O5/served 1-4 years/Deployed 3-5 times/Iraq, State Side)

"That life is all about changes, and that to be prepared, you need to always be ready for anything."—**A.U.**, Air Force; Served 5-10 years; Deployed 3-5 times; Married; Father.

What 3 things have you learned in the process that you wish someone had shared with you?
One: your employer may not expect you to be a great leader.
Two: your employer may see you as an emotional liability.
Three: your employer may see you as unable to work independently. My advice: show them (your employers) otherwise. As veteran service members we have all be trained to be great leaders, to be steadfast and levelheaded and to excel independently. We bring strength and structure to any workforce. I live my life by the air force motto, INTEGRITY FIRST SERVICE BEFORE SELF EXCELLENCE IN ALL WE DO!"—**Jason M.**

For more questions and responses, or to complete the employment survey yourself in order to share your thoughts, feelings and advice with other service members, visit www.civilianside.com

****
A Resumé Improvement Workshop!

On the following pages are two resumés I've helped improve. Use them to gain practice recognizing what elements of your own resumé can be improved.

GI Jane Page 1: BEFORE

GI Jane

2014 Transition Blvd Jacksonville, FL, 76543   480-678-1240   gijane2014@yahoo.com

CAREER SUMMARY:
Accomplished and highly motivated United States Army veteran with over two decades of expertise in leadership and management roles. Possess strong interpersonal skills with ability to establish rapport at all levels. Organized and disciplined, able to multitask, prioritize, and achieve organizational objectives and deadlines in diverse and challenging environments. Maintain Top Secret Security Clearance with Sensitive Compartmented Information (SCI).

AREAS OF EXPERTISE

LEADERSHIP	SUPERVISION	TRAINING & DEVELOPMENT	PERSONNEL MANAGEMENT	ADMINISTRATION
HUMAN RESOURCE MANAGEMENT / STAFFING		PERSONNEL RULES / POLICIES / REGULATIONS		OPERATIONS
PROGRAM MANAGEMENT		PLANNING / BUDGETING	BRIEFINGS / PRESENTATIONS	
COMMUNICATION: ORAL AND WRITTEN		STRATEGIC ANALYSIS	DECISION MAKING	TEAM BUILDING

PROFESSIONAL EXPERIENCE:

Chief, Special Actions Branch/Human Capital Core Enterprise Liaison Officer   January 2010-Present
2nd Battalion G-1   Fort Campbell, KY

- Demonstrated expertise directing Army Reserve Headquarters and subordinate units with guidance, policy, and oversight involving key human resources and command management programs.
- Proficiently oversee command's Congressional/Special Inquiry Program.
- Accountable for providing Army Reserve leadership with administrative support services, and coordinated near, short, and long term operations and strategic communications.
- Extracted Human Capital Core Enterprise's equities from All-Army Activities, published operations orders, reviewed and responded to General Officers' taskers, and managed military personnel initiatives to prepare weekly human resources metrics.
- Diligently prepared weekly briefings for Director of Human Capital Core Enterprise to present assessment updates to Deputy Commanding General Officers in operations and support for vital decision-making.
- Recognized as lead Crisis Actions Officer developed Human Capital Core Enterprise Contingency Operations Plan implemented during natural disasters, and national security issues in United States and overseas.

Deputy/Senior Human Resources Officer   June 2008 July 2010
3rd Legal Command   Ft. Drum, NY

- Distinguished Deputy/Senior Human Resources Manager for United States Army Legal Command, directed command of 28 Colonel Commands covering United States and territories.
- Successfully oversaw daily operational functions of Human Resources staff.
- Subject matter expert in human resources management and personnel administration to enhance Reserve Component Judge Advocate's Corps (JAG) personnel readiness.
- Advised Legal Command's Commanding General and staff on personnel regulations, policies and procedures, personnel accountability, personnel status reporting, while managing human resources actions.

Deputy Director of the United States North Region   April 2006-May 2008
National Committee for Employer Support of the Guard and Reserve   Ft Hood, TX

- Accomplished West Regional Deputy Director of 15 states within United States, including: Alaska, Hawaii, American Samoa, Guam and Saipan, while under Director of Committee Support Operations, joint service activity for Office of Assistant Secretary of Defense for Reserve Affairs.
- Instrumental in directing 1,025 volunteers and full-time staff for largest and most diverse region to gain and maintain employer support of Air/National Guard and Reserve Components during unprecedented mobilizations and deployments.
- Valued Project Officer for Western Regional Conferences deployed new Planning, Execution, and Performance Report Systems for 56 field committees under National Committee for Employer Support of Guard and Reserve.

GI Jane Page 2: BEFORE

GI Jane   Page 2   gijane2014@yahoo.com

Deputy Director of the United States West Region (CONTINUED)   April 2006-May 2008
National Committee for Employer Support of the Guard and Reserve   Ft Hood, TX

- Meticulously provided national committee data roll-ups serving as basis for Employer Support of Guard and Reserve's Annual Reports used for Congressional testimonies, Department of Defense decision making, and garnering employer support of employees who were members of Guard and Reserve.

Human Resources Strategic Plans Officer   June 2004-Mar 2006
Office of the Chief of the Army Reserve   Ft Lewis, Washington

- Successfully served as Accessions Planning Officer for United States Army Reserve, and selected as project manager to develop and implement program management, oversight, policy, and guidance on all initiatives and actions affecting military human resource requirements in areas of recruitment, initial training, and retention within Army Reserve.
- Effectively represented Human Resources Directorate at Army-level meetings and liaisons with joint forces to ensure Army Reserve accession initiatives and equities were achieved to meet Congressionally-mandated end strength objective of 205K Soldiers.
- Proficiently conducted primary analysis for Army Reserve's personnel programs, and forecasted impact of policy changes prior to and after implementation of strategic initiatives and objectives to support Officer of Secretary of Defense and Congressional leadership.

Chief, United States Army Element Branch   May 2002-June 2004
United States North East Command   Ft. Hamilton, NY

- Liaised with representatives from Northeast Command directorates and sub-unified commands to manage 2,600+ reserve authorizations.
- Effective Project Manager for Reserve forces structure for Army, Army National Guard, Air Force, Navy, and Marines at four-star headquarters.
- Strategically directed mobilizations, personnel actions, and assignments for Army Element and Army Reserve detachments.
- Established Pacific Command's liaison representative for Joint Staff, Department of Defense, Department of Army and Army Human Resources Commands.

EDUCATION AND TRAINING:

PhD Candidate, Human Resource Management, DeVry University
M.S.A., Business Administration, UMUC, 1994
B. S., Communication, Albany State University, 1985
Command and General Staff College, Fort Leavenworth, Kansas, 2001
Human Resources Management Qualification Course, Alexander, Virginia, 1999
Combined Arms Staff College, Fort Leavenworth, Kansas, 1995

EDUCATION AND TRAINING (CONTINUED):

United States Army Recruiting Operations Officer School, Fort Benjamin Harrison, Indiana, 1992
Officer Advanced Course, Fort Eustis, Virginia, 1990
Officer Basic Course, Fort Benjamin Harrison, Indiana 1985

Recipient of Numerous Military Awards

TECHNOLOGY SKILLS:

Proficient in: Microsoft Office (Word, Excel, PowerPoint, Access); Microsoft SharePoint; Macintosh Operating Systems

GI Jane Page 1: AFTER

GI Jane

2014 Transition Blvd Jacksonville, FL, 76543   480-678-1240   gijane2014@yahoo.com

PROFESSIONAL SUMMARY

Quality and results oriented leader with more than 20 years of experience operating at various levels of the Military. Relationship builder who quickly establishes rapport and motivate teams to accomplish goals. Out of the box thinker with advanced communication skills and intensive understanding of creating effective business strategies. Skilled facilitator with strong organizational, project management multi-task skills.

PROFESSIONAL EXPERIENCE:

Director of Human Resources Special Actions Division January 2010-Present
Human Resources Department Fort Campbell, KY

- Demonstrated expertise directing Army Reserve Headquarters and subordinate units with guidance, policy, and oversight involving key human resources and command management programs.
- Action officer oversee and responded to and resolved over 2000 command's United States Congressional/Presidential Special Inquiries.
- Provided Army Reserve leadership with administrative support services. Developed and coordinated short and long term operations and strategic communications affecting 205,000 reservists worldwide.
- Diligently prepared weekly briefings for Director of Human Capital Core Enterprise to present assessment updates to Deputy Commanding General Officers in operations and support for vital decision-making.
- Lead Crisis Actions Officer, developed Contingency Operations Plan implemented during natural disasters and national security issues worldwide.

Assistant Human Resources Director June 2008 July 2010
3rd Legal Command Ft. Drum, NY

- Activated United States Army Legal Command and provided human resources services to 28 Senior Officers Commands total customer population of 1752 dispersed throughout United States.
- Accounted for daily operational functions of Human Resources staff of 28.
- Served as advisor to the Commanding General and staff on Human Resources related issues regarding updated personnel regulations, policies and procedures, on personnel accountability and status reporting.

Deputy Director of the United States West Region April 2006-May 2008
National Committee for Employer Support of the Guard and Reserve Ft Hood, TX

- West Regional Deputy Director of 15 states, to include: Alaska, Hawaii, American Samoa, Guam and Saipan.
- Directing 1,025 volunteers and full-time staff for largest and most diverse region to gain and maintain employer support of Air/National Guard and Reserve Components during unprecedented mobilizations and deployments.
- Project Officer for 15 Western Regional Conferences developed and deployed new Planning, Execution, and Performance Report Systems for 56 field committees worldwide.

Human Resources Strategic Plans Officer June 2004-Mar 2006
 Ft Lewis, Washington

- Accessions Planning Officer for United States Army Reserve, and selected as project manager to develop and implement program management, oversight, policy, and guidance on all initiatives and actions affecting military human resource requirements in areas of recruitment, initial training, and retention within Army Reserve.
- Human Resources liaison at Army-level meetings with joint forces to ensure Army Reserve accession initiatives were achieved to meet Congressionally-mandated end strength objective of 205,000 Soldiers.
- Conducted strength, weakness, opportunity and threat (SWOT) analysis for Army Reserve's personnel programs. Identified and forecasted impact of federal policy changes prior to and after implementation of strategic initiatives.

GI Jane Page 2: AFTER

> GI Jane Page 2 gijane2014@yahoo.com
>
> **Chief, United States Army Element Branch** May 2002-June 2004
> **United States North East Command** Ft. Hamilton, NY
>
> - Liaised with representatives from Pacific Command directorates and sub-unified commands to manage 2,600+ reserve authorizations.
> - Effective Project Manager for Reserve forces structure for Army, Army National Guard, Air Force, Navy, and Marines at four-star headquarters to provide essential human resources command and control of U.S. military forces, during peace and wartime.
> - Strategically directed mobilizations, personnel actions, and assignments for Army Element and Army Reserve detachments.
> - Established Pacific Command's liaison representative for United States Joint Staff, Department of Defense, Department of Army and Army Human Resources Commands.
>
> **EDUCATION AND TRAINING:**
>
> M.S.A., Business Administration, UMUC, 1994
> B. S., Communication, Albany State University
> Senior Leader Staff College, Fort Leavenworth, Kansas
> Human Resources Management Qualification Course, Alexandria, Virginia
> United States Army Recruiting Operations Officer School, Fort Benjamin Harrison, Indiana
> Advanced Leadership Course, Fort Eustis, Virginia
> Officer Basic Leadership Course, Fort Benjamin Harrison, Indiana
> Lean Six Sigma – White Belt, Fort Bragg, North Carolina
> Contracting Officer Representative Course, United States Army Logistics University, Fort Lee, Virginia
>
> **TECHNOLOGY SKILLS:**
>
> Proficient in: Microsoft Office Suite; Microsoft SharePoint; Macintosh Operating Systems

Changes made:

1- reworded summary; changed two decades to 20 years,
2- removed security clearance
3- removed area of expertise as this will be covered in professional summary
4- reworded job titles; quantified accomplishments; 3-4 bullets per position
5- removed education that has not been earned
6- combined with section 4; removed "recipient of numerous awards"
7- reworded skills "Proficient in Microsoft Office Suite" instead of listing each individual application

This is how our next case study, Navy Betty, submitted her resumé to me:

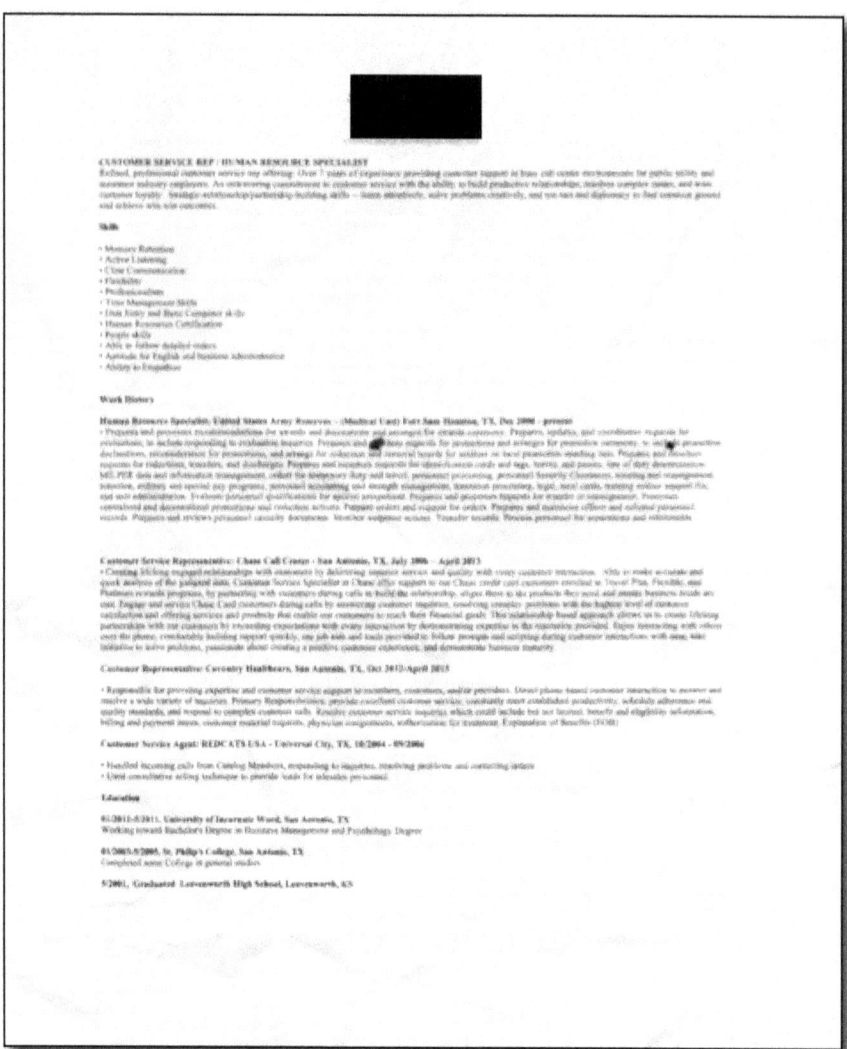

For the purpose of legibility, I'll transcribe it on the following page

Navy Betty (BEFORE)
270 Thousand Oaks, Apt 1322Q
Dallas, TX 97832
Cell: (400) 258-9999
navybetty@gmail.com

CUSTOMER SERVICE REP / HUMAN RESOURCE SPECIALIST
Refined, professional customer service rep offering: Over 7 years of experience providing customer support in busy call center environments for public utility and insurance industry employers. An unwavering commitment to customer service with the ability to build productive relationships, resolves complex issues, and wins customer loyalty. Strategic-relationship/partnership-building skills -- listen attentively, solve problems creatively, and use tact and diplomacy to find common ground and achieve win-win outcomes.

- Memory Retention
- Active Listening
- Clear Communication
- Flexibility
- Professionalism
- Time Management Skills

- Data Entry/Computer skills
- Human Resources Certification
- People Skills

- Able to follow orders
- Aptitude for English and business administration
- Ability to Empathize

Human Resource Specialist; United States Army Reserves (Medical Unit) Fort Sam Houston, TX, Dec 2000 – present
• Prepares and processes recommendations for awards and decorations and arranges for awards ceremony. Prepares, updates, and coordinates requests for evaluations, to include responding to evaluation inquiries. Prepares and monitors requests for promotions and arranges for promotion ceremony, to include promotion declinations, reconsideration for promotions, and arrange for reduction and removal boards for soldiers on local promotion standing lists. Prepares and monitors requests for reductions, transfers, and discharges. Prepares and monitors requests for identification cards and tags, leaves, and passes, line of duty determination, MILPER data and information management, orders for temporary duty and travel, personnel processing, personnel Security Clearances, training and reassignment, retention, military and special pay programs, personnel accounting and strength management, transition processing, legal, meal cards, training soldier support file, and unit administration. Evaluate personnel qualifications for special assignment. Prepares and processes requests for transfer or reassignment. Processes centralized and decentralized promotions and reduction actions. Prepare orders and request for orders. Prepares and maintains officer and enlisted personnel records. Prepares and reviews personnel casualty documents. Monitor suspense actions. Transfer records. Process personnel for separations and retirements

Customer Service Representative: Chase Call Center - San Antonio, TX, July 2006 – April 2013
• Creating lifelong engaged relationships with customers by delivering superior service and quality with every customer interaction. I am able to make accurate and quick analysis of the gathered data. Customer Service Specialist at Chase offer support to our Chase credit card customers enrolled in Travel Plus, Flexible, and Platinum rewards

programs, by partnering with customers during calls to build the relationship, aligns them to the products they need and ensure business needs are met. Engage and service Chase Card customers during calls by answering customer inquiries, resolving complex problems with the highest level of customer satisfaction and offering services and products that enable our customers to reach their financial goals. This relationship-based approach allows us to create lifelong partnerships with our customers by exceeding expectations with every interaction by demonstrating expertise in the resolution provided. Enjoy interacting with others over the phone, comfortable building rapport quickly, use job aids and tools provided to follow prompts and scripting during customer interactions with ease, take initiative to solve problems, passionate about creating a positive customer experience, and demonstrate business maturity.

Customer Representative: Coventry Healthcare, San Antonio, TX, Oct 2012-April 2013
- Responsible for providing expertise and customer service support to members, customers, and/or providers. Direct phone-based customer interaction to answer and resolve a wide variety of inquiries. Primary Responsibilities; provide excellent customer service, constantly meet established productivity, schedule adherence and quality standards, and respond to complex customer calls. Resolve customer service inquiries which could include but not limited: benefit and eligibility information, billing and payment issues, customer material requests, physician assignments, authorization for treatment, Explanation of Benefits (EOB)

Customer Service Agent: REDCATS USA - Universal City, TX, 10/2004 - 09/2006
- Handled incoming calls from Catalog Members, responding to inquiries, resolving problems and correcting orders.
- Used consultative selling technique to provide leads for telesales personnel.

01/2003-5/2005, St. Philip's College, 01/2011-5/2011, University of Incarnate Word, San Antonio, TX
Completed some College in general studies

5/2001, Graduated Leavenworth High School, Leavenworth, KS

Chief Raymond's Edits:

1. Use font size of at least 11 or 12
2. Use professional reworded summary instead of current title.
3. Remove skills sections; it should be covered on the summary
4. Change the title, use bullets and quantify. Unit doesn't matter
5. Use bullets and quantifiable accomplishments
6. Remove education that has not been earned

Navy Betty (AFTER)
270 Thousand Oaks, Apt 1322Q
Dallas, TX 97832
Cell: (400) 258-9999
navybetty@gmail.com

PROFESSIONAL SUMMARY:
Results oriented Human Resources professional and customer relations manager. Challenged driven leader and complex problem solver who overcomes obstacles and deliver results. Relationship builder who quickly establishes rapport and motivate teams to accomplish goals. Out of box thinker able to develop and implement effective business strategies and creative win-win solutions. Skilled communicator with strong interpersonal and multi-task skills.

Work History

Human Resource Generalist, United States Army Reserves – Fort Sam Houston, TX, Dec 2000 – present

- Prepared and processed more than 150 awards for more than 450 soldiers geographically dispersed throughout 7 states
- Project Manager for more than 15 ceremonies
- Provided human resources services for more than 450 soldiers geographically located throughout 7 states.

Customer Service Representative: Chemical Bank Call Center - San Antonio, TX, July 2006 – April 2013

- Fielded more than 300 calls daily resolving more than 85% of customers issues
- Served as Chemical Bank Call center lead customer service representative
- Recommended customer improvement solutions to better serve the customer and reduce time spent on the telephone resulting in increased productivity for the team

Customer Representative: Coventry Healthcare, San Antonio, TX, Oct 2012-April 2013

- Subject matter customer service representative providing service to members, customers, and providers.
- Consistently exceeded established productivity goals, quality standards. Resolved daily on average 17 complex customer calls including billing and payment
- Liaison with physicians authorized payments for treatment and thoroughly explained recommended customer improvement solutions to better serve the customer and reduce time for issuance of members' benefits.

Customer Service Agent: REDCATS USA - Universal City, TX, 10/2004 - 09/2006
- Used sales techniques gaining more than 60 new leads per month for telesales team increasing monthly sales by 25 %
- Successfully handled more than 80 calls per day from catalog members, responding, resolving problems, and correcting orders.

Education
01/2003-5/2005 Human Resources Training, Columbia, SC Fort Jackson

6/2007- 8/23/2007 Advanced Leadership training

01/2011-3/2011 Customer Service Training

5/2001 Graduated Leavenworth High School, Leavenworth, KS

Samples of Federal Resumés

Forget what you know about typical resumé writing. While you may find yourself summarizing your work history into a one-page document for a typical job application, your federal resumé should be more detailed and run two-to-five pages in length for an entry-level job. A federal resumé uses the same information from a typical resumé, but goes into more depth about your skills, past duties and accomplishments.—**GoGovernment.org**

[The following is courtesy of FederalResumeWriter.com]
This *resumé* runs 7 pages in its original form.—Chief Raymond

ADMINISTRATIVE OFFICER (Director of Management and Operations Overseas), FP-0341-04/02

STEPHEN HAWKMAN
543 Hudson Lane
Gridley, CA 95948
Home Phone: 000-765-3334
Cell Phone: 000-765-2110
Email: hawkman@sbcglobal.net

US Citizen
Veteran's Preference: 5 points, U.S. Air Force, 06/1980 to 08/2004
Highest Previous Grade: N/A
Security Clearance: Top Secret, SCI clearance (active)

PROFESSIONAL PROFILE

Highly innovative and results-oriented professional with proven track record for developing and implementing effective plans, managing diverse programs, meeting targets and exceeding goals. Practiced in budget development and administration. Experience in applying analytical and evaluative methods to assess the efficiency and effectiveness of programs and recommend changes as appropriate. Resourceful thinker, problem solver and decision maker. Ability to interpret and ensure compliance of applicable regulations, guidelines, policies and procedures. Proven skill in developing, administering and managing training programs. Outstanding communication skills, including proficiency at writing complex analyses and preparing reports, and superior ability to communicate in a multi-cultural environment with individuals at all levels.

PROFESSIONAL HISTORY

08/2006 to present, SUBSTITUTE TEACHER, Campbell Elementary School District, Grades K-8, Farris, CA, 08/2008 – present; Farris Unified School District, Grades 9-12, Farris, CA, 08/2007 – present; Davis Unified School District, Grades K-12, Davis, CA, 08/2006 to present, $100 per day, Brad Taylor, 530-846-5888; Maria Smith (Davis), 530- 846-4222; Marjorie Long, 530-695-9950, Contact: yes.

PERFORM ON-CALL SUBSTITUTE TEACHING for elementary and secondary school students in various subjects. Facilitate learning with lecture and active discussion. Advise and guide students regarding supplemental resources to enhance knowledge. Assign readings and homework. Ensure learning goals and objectives are consistently met.

DEMONSTRATE HIGHLY DEVELOPED COMMUNICATIONS SKILLS. Interact with students in class discussions and provide assistance and guidance with course content and lessons.

ACCOMPLISHMENTS: Many teachers like the way I handle their classes as a substitute teacher and request me by name when they need a substitute; recognized for dependability in following curriculum and interfacing and working effectively with diverse students.

08/2009 to 01/2010, INTERN MATH TEACHER, Inderkum High School, Sacramento, CA 95835, 40 hours per week, $44,000 per year, Janet Mann, Vice Principal, 916-567- 5640, Contact: yes.

PROVIDED CLASSROOM INSTRUCTION in four classes of Algebra 1 and one class of Geometry to ethnically diverse students in grades 9 through 12. Effectively managed classrooms. Developed individualized motivational strategies to reach students with varied learning styles. Assigned homework, prepared tests, reviewed and graded homework and unit tests. Interpreted and applied school policies to all teaching and administrative activities.

USED EXCELLENT INTERPERSONAL AND TRAINING SKILLS to provide classroom instruction to students with various learning styles and levels of understanding. Regularly communicated progress and concerns to school administrators, teachers, other staff and parents. Made recommendations for improvements. Engaged in outreach to parents, conducted parent teacher conferences, promoted parental involvement and participation.

DEVELOPED AND IMPLEMENTED CREATIVE COURSE LESSON PLANS AND TESTS. Researched, analyzed and evaluated new studies and information, and updated curriculum as needed. Prepared and distributed supplemental course materials to enhance learning.

ACCOMPLISHMENTS: Inderkum High School is rated the second most ethnically/culturally diverse high school in the nation. I used the Spanish language extensively to keep parents apprised of student progress and behavior. I established incentive rewards and competition between classes to motivate students to do their homework and take their education seriously. As a result of my efforts, student pass rate for Algebra 1 increased from 60% to 83%.

09/2008 to 09/2009, INTERN MATH TEACHER (7th Grade), Leroy Gray Middle School, Elk Grove, CA 95634, 40 hours per week, $44,000 per year, David Evans, Principal, 916-502-5560, Contact: yes.

INSTRUCTED, ADVISED AND COUNSELED students in Intervention Math. Managed classroom activities for classes with 108 seventh grade students, providing practical application of subject matter. Assessed student performance, counseled on learning objectives and assigned grades for completed coursework. Interpreted and applied school policies to all teaching and administrative activities.

CONSISTENTLY DISPLAYED EXCELLENT ORAL AND WRITTEN COMMUNICATIONS SKILLS. Interacted with students on a daily basis in active class discussion. Met with students individually to provide assistance as well as respond to questions and concerns. Regularly communicated progress and concerns to school administrators, teachers, other staff and parents. Participated in faculty meetings to discuss ideas and issues; provided recommendations for educational program improvements. Designed and developed complex course curriculum. Wrote detailed lesson plans and class syllabus. Developed, drafted and distributed correspondence, reports and other documentation in the performance of duties.

ACCOMPLISHMENTS:
Pioneered a new intervention course called "Fast Forward Math." Peer teachers, the math department head and the principal of the school all lauded my use of PowerPoint slideshows with animation for teaching math concepts.

Taught intervention math to seventh grade students, 95% of whom were ethnic minorities. Used Spanish language to effectively communicate student progress/behavior with parents of Latino students. Established incentive rewards (homework passes, pizza party, game days) to motivate students to do their homework and take their education seriously.

06/1980 to 08/2004, COMMUNICATIONS AND INFORMATION SYSTEMS OFFICER and FOREIGN AREA OFFICER-LATIN AMERICA (Lieutenant Colonel); U.S. Air Force, Pentagon, Arlington, VA 20330, 40+ hours per week, $108,000 per year, Craig Dobson, (703) 693-1281, Contact: yes.

PLANNED, ADMINISTERED, DIRECTED AND MANAGED SEVERAL MULTI- MILLION DOLLAR ACQUISITION, OPERATIONS AND MAINTENANCE, BASE SUPPORT AND COMMUNICATIONS SYSTEMS SUPPORT PROJECTS AND PROGRAMS; included plan, schedule and layout of operations, planning for budget and cost requirements and supervising program staff. Participated in developing and implementing long- and short-range plans, procedures and policies relating to the specific organization's program and administrative needs. For various assignments, worked with staff in a multi-cultural environment to set annual performance goals for organization. Organized and integrated logistics functions to achieve communications and information support mission accomplishment. Prepared and executed procurement actions for communications and information technology systems, in accordance with Federal Acquisitions Regulation (FAR), USAF and DoD contracting rules and procedures.

DEVELOPED, DIRECTED, ADMINISTERED AND MANAGED EDUCATION/TRAINING PROGRAMS. While assigned as an Exchange Officer in Brazil and Mexico, provided program and administrative management and support to several educational institutions. Developed, or assisted with development, of curriculum; taught classes. Ensured innovative processes were used in developing training competencies, learning objectives and evaluation techniques. Determined scope, objectives and methods of training. Used adult learning principles to develop graduate level computer science curriculum for Brazilian Air Force's Institute of Aeronautical Technology, while serving as Scientific and Engineering Exchange Officer.

PROVIDED LEADERSHIP, TECHNICAL ADVICE, GUIDANCE AND ASSISTANCE regarding programs or policies. Provided advice to management and program personnel on budgetary and finance issues such as budget formulation, justification and execution, and financial management. While assigned as Director, Logistics and Engineering at McClellan AFB, served as principal advisor regarding logistics for sensor systems deployed internationally for detection and characterization of weapons of mass destruction. While serving as Deputy Commander, 77th Support Group at McClellan AFB, formulated a base closure plan and provided administrative and logistical guidance for divestiture of all buildings and resources. While assigned as Deputy Director of Communications at Soto Cano Air Base in Honduras, offered leadership advice to manager of Hondutel telephone switch regarding how to establish critical communications links for demining and medical teams. Continuously served as a resource for technical program advice and assistance. While serving as Exchange Officer- English Language Instructor in Guadalajara, Mexico, provided leadership advice and assistance to superintendent and principal to build and sustain community-based development / educational program that provided Mexican national students the opportunity to receive an education based on U.S. culture, customs and academic standards.

Rucksack to Briefcase 143

PLANNED, FORMULATED, EXECUTED, MANAGED AND ANALYZED BUDGETS for acquisition, operations and maintenance, base support, communications systems support and educational program support; provided administrative support and guidance for organizational budgeting and financial management activities. Communicated with program personnel to perform cost benefit evaluations of current and projected programs; identified funding requirements to support operations; prepared detailed analyses and estimates of funding needs and submitted to leadership for approval. Administered, tracked, monitored and analyzed approved budgets. Prepared financial analysis and budget reports.

INTERPRETED AND APPLIED USAF, DOD AND COMMAND ORDERS, INSTRUCTIONS, DIRECTIVES, POLICIES, PROCEDURES AND REGULATIONS to program and administrative functions, activities and issues. Provided technical and procedural guidance regarding programs to all involved personnel. Determined applicability and effect of new or proposed policies, executive orders or agency directives on operations and program requirements.

APPLIED ANALYTICAL AND EVALUATIVE METHODS AND TECHNIQUES to ASSESS PROGRAM EFFECTIVENESS AND EFFICIENCY in supporting operations and contributing to organizational objectives and goals. Identified issues, problems or deficiencies; prepared recommendations for changing methods and practices in order to enhance operations. Analyzed and ensured all program operations were in compliance with established regulations, procedures, sound management practices and effective use of staff. Gathered key information, compiled reports, provided analysis and maintained program files.

LED, SUPERVISED AND PROVIDED GUIDANCE AND INSTRUCTION to multi- national military and civilian engineers, technicians and other program personnel. Assigned work according to program and leadership priorities. Ensured on-going performance management, creating a partnership to work towards resolution of program issues or concerns. Provided counsel and advice to employees on work and administrative matters. Developed work improvement plans and implemented new approaches or changes in work processes and procedures. Ensured accomplishment of goals of equal employment opportunity (EEO) by adhering to nondiscriminatory practices.

INTERACTED WITH A WIDE RANGE OF PERSONNEL, USING EFFECTIVE INTERPERSONAL SKILLS; continually built and maintained effective partnerships and professional networks to support programs and policies. Developed and maintained relationships with organizational leadership, program personnel, government officials and other stakeholders to foster coalition building and cooperation in accomplishing program goals and objectives. Participated in meetings and conference calls, presented program reports, recommendations and solutions, addressed administrative issues and exchanged information about program activities with all levels of personnel.

DEVELOPED NUMEROUS DOCUMENTS AND REPORTS to support program and administrative operations. Collected program data and developed reports with analytical findings and recommendations. Developed, collected, analyzed and updated budget and financial data in spreadsheets and databases; compiled data and created reports with complex tables, graphs and charts using Word, Excel and PowerPoint. Used electronic mail system to prepare, distribute and respond to critical correspondence.

ACCOMPLISHMENTS:

05/2002 – 08/2004, Chief, Communications-Electronics Branch, Pentagon, Washington DC - Prepared, executed and managed $1.8 billion communications-electronics (C-E) budget for USAF. Justified and defended C-E funding requests through Air Force senior leadership, Office of the Secretary of Defense, Office of Management and Budget, and Congress.

02/1999 – 05/2002, Chief, Network Domain Support Branch, Norfolk, VA - Assigned to North Atlantic Treaty Organization (NATO). Managed $4 million operations and maintenance budget. Supervised 50 multi-national communications and information systems engineers and technicians (from Canada and several European countries) supporting systems in North America and Europe. Guided this team of professionals to establish and/or maintain connection of fourteen multinational ships and four satellite ground terminal sites to NATO's WAN. Worked collaboratively with three foreign national Section Chiefs, to determine long-range work plans and set annual performance goals for our organization. Built effective partnership with NATO's C3 Agency, aligning priorities to perform tests jointly to ensure WAN routers were Y2K compliant.

08/1998 – 02/1999, Deputy Commander, 77th Support Group, Travis AFB, CA - Led 1,023 military and civilian personnel in Communications Squadron, Security Police Squadron, Mission Support Squadron, and Services Division. Led and managed community enhancement and development projects for base and retiree personnel, including those that involved computer/communications, small businesses/restaurants, youth care and education and more. Managed $12 million annual base support budget. Formulated base closure plan, including divestiture of buildings and resources valued at $2.1 billion.

08/1997 – 08/1998, Director, Logistics and Engineering, Travis AFB, CA - Supervised 90 logisticians, engineers and technicians. Directed life cycle management of $65 million sensor systems deployed worldwide for detection and characterization of weapons of mass destruction. Provided flawless logistics support for critical airborne sampling operations against India and Pakistan nuclear tests.

12/1996 – 08/1997, Director, Mission Resources and Systems, Travis AFB, CA - Supervised 26 person staff in the Communications-Computer Division. Flawlessly executed $4.5 million in procurement actions. Managed $7.3 million operations and maintenance budget. Planned and implemented $475,000 local area network replacement, increasing data transfer rates 20-fold and doubling reliability.

12/1994 – 06/1995, Deputy Director of Communications, Soto Cano Air Base, Honduras, Central America - Managed $6 million communications support contract for Joint Task Force Bravo. Negotiated support from a U.S. contractor to install 50 new telephone lines at no charge to the government. Using expert Spanish skills, built and managed team in a multi-cultural environment; coordinated efforts of Honduran telecommunications companies, contractors, technicians, and U.S. military technicians to establish critical communications links for de-mining and medical teams, enhancing survivability of Joint Forces in Central America, and supporting economic development / building operations in Honduras.

05/1989 – 05/1992, Exchange Officer-English Language Instructor, Guadalajara, Mexico - Served as member of the school board for the American School, grades K through 12 for 2.5 years. Provided leadership advice and assistance to the superintendent and principal with respect to curriculum development, budget approval, facilities management, hiring of faculty members and student discipline. - Directed English Language Instruction program at Mexican Air Force Academy, preparing 171 cadets for aerospace studies. Taught many classes of English as a foreign language. Directed 12 Mexican instructors in teaching technical English to cadets; built team cohesion by getting to know instructors through association outside of normal work hours.

06/1984 – 06/1986, Scientific and Engineering Exchange Officer, Brazil - Selected to participate in a President-initiated program as the first Scientific and Engineering Exchange Officer to Brazil. While assigned to the Brazilian Air Force's Institute of Aeronautical Technology, pioneered graduate level computer science curriculum; taught courses in Portuguese.

08/1974 to 10/1976, Volunteer Missionary, Church of Jesus Christ of Latter-day Saints, Buenos Aires, Argentina

Held key leadership positions of Zone Leader and Assistant to the Mission President: While serving as Zone Leader for eight months, responsible for logistics of missionary training conferences. While serving as Assistant to the Mission President for four months, managed vaccination program for 150 missionaries, personally applying injections to keep missionaries healthy and protected.

EDUCATION

2009, Degree: Single Subject Teaching Credential, State of Arizon, Sun City West, CA, 41 quarter hours, Area of Concentration: Foundation-Level Mathematics
1982, Master of Science Degree, Air Force Institute of Technology, Wright-Patterson AFB, OH, 70 quarter hours, Major: Information Systems, GPA: 3.82; Distinguished Graduate

1980, Bachelor of Science Degree, Baley University, Provo, UT, 136.5 semester hours, Major: Computer Science, GPA: 3.53

1973, Manteca High School, Manteca, CA, High School Diploma

LICENSURES AND CERTIFICATIONS

Single Subject Teaching Credential, State of Arizona, 2009, Area of Concentration: Foundation-Level Mathematics

MILITARY TRAINING

Air War College (correspondence course), 2000, Air University, Travis AFB, one year
Joint Command and Warfare Staff Officer Course, Armed Forces Staff College, 1999
Fundamentals of Systems Acquisition Management, 1996
General Hazard Communication Training Program, 1996
Air Command and Staff College (by seminar), 1994
Harvard Graphics 3.0 Familiarization, 1993
Advanced Communications-Computer Officer Training Course, 1992
Automated Information Systems Project Management, 1987

Space Operations Orientation, 1987
Squadron Officers School, 1987,
Air University, Maxwell AFB, nine weeks Brazilian Portuguese Language Training, 1984
Defense Language Institute, six months Introduction to Digital Communications, 1982
Spread Spectrum Communication Systems, 1982
Digital Signal Processing, 1982

AWARDS, HONORS, RECOGNITION
Meritorious Service Medal with four Bronze Oak Leaf Clusters, 2004, 1999, 1996, 1993, and 1986
Defense Meritorious Service Medal, 2002
National Defense Service Medal with one Bronze Star, 2002 and 1995
Air Force Longevity Service Award with four Bronze Oak Leaf Clusters, 2000, 1996, 1992, 1988, and 1984
Air Force Achievement Medal with one Bronze Oak Leaf Cluster, 1999 and 1984 Joint Service Achievement Medal, 1995
Air Force Overseas Long Tour Ribbon with one Bronze Oak Leaf Cluster, 1992 and 1986
Air Force Commendation Medal, 1989
Distinguished Graduate, Defense Language Institute, 1984
Martin Kellogg Award, Defense Language Institute, 1984
Distinguished Graduate, Air Force Institute of Technology, 1982

PROFESSIONAL MEMBERSHIPS AND AFFILIATIONS

Tau Beta Pi National Engineering Honor Society, since 1981

MILITARY SERVICE
U.S. Air Force, 06/1979 to 08/2003, Honorable Discharge
Overseas Assignments: Brazil (two years), Mexico (three years), Honduras (six months), Colombia (six months)

SPECIAL SKILLS Type 45+ WPM

LANGUAGES: Spanish: fluent – read, write, speak; Brazilian Portuguese: low to intermediate fluency Lived and worked for eight years in five different Latin American Countries

Mrs Chief (Federal Resume 2)

41 Virginia Drive• Bastion City, Texas • (000) 654-9999
Email:mrschief@gmail.com

SUMMARY
A goal-oriented and dedicated team leader with more than 20 years of experience in education and training. Exceptional Instructional Leader looking forward to utilizing acquired knowledge in an Education Leadership position.

EDUCATION
Masters of Science - Education Administration, S.U.N.Y Albany, New York
Masters of Science - Urban Education, Cambridge College, Massachusetts
Bachelor of Art - Communications, S.U.N.Y at Oswego, New York

CERTIFICATIONS
Principal	Texas
Teacher K-6	New York
School/District Administrator	New York

LEADERSHIP/SUPERVISORY EXPERIENCE

Consultant/Academic Director of Koinonia Community Learning Academy, Houston, TX
Supervisor: Stephanie Smith (949) 123.4678
Hours: 40/per week
7/2010-11/2010
Supervised and managed the day to day activities of the staff and facilities. Co-labored in formulating the school's mission and faculty/students handbook. Co-chaired the Leadership Team and collaborated with members to create and enforce the school's comprehensive education plan. Established and monitored the execution of educational goals, policies and procedures for the school community. Planned, created and implemented new curricula and academic programs. Developed a professional development program to support the implementation of the new curriculum initiative. Recruited, interviewed and employed highly qualified staff. Developed data analysis teams to evaluate and track students' educational progress and performance. Completed informal/formal evaluations of teachers' performance. Allocated and monitored expenditure of the school's budget.

Learning Community Instructional Leader, Community Education Partners, 1999 Beechnut Street, Houston, TX 77074, (765) 000-1995,

Supervisor: Stephanie Smith (949) 000.4678
Hours: 40/per week
8/2006-8/2008
Collaborated with the school wide leadership team in aggregating data to analyze, evaluate and address school wide issues and students' performance. Managed and supervised the daily operation of staff, students and facility. Supervised and evaluated the performance of the instructional staff. Supervised and monitored the implementation of curriculum and the impact on students' performance. Trained and supported instructional staff in the implementation of best teaching practices. Developed and implemented professional development plans for instructional staff and monitored the impact on students' performance. Facilitated weekly meetings with staff to review educational goals and objectives for students. Implemented the students' code of conduct and enforced disciplinary actions. Maintained and monitored up to date students' academic goals and behavioral management plans. Liaison between staff, parents and the school community on behavioral and educational issues. Coordinated and implemented school policies and procedures. Advocated for reformed school policies and programs to meet students' needs. Established and ensured the accuracy of students' attendance and academic records.

PROFESSIONAL DEVELOPMENT/TRAINING EXPERIENCE

Facilitator/Consultant, United Federation of Teachers, 100 Broadway, New York, NY 10004
Supervisor: Maryanne Gilligan (917) 000.1234
Hours: 35-50/per week
10/2002-8/2005
Maintained and operated a professional development site for the district/region. Served as the consultant and site coordinator for the regional professional development center. Analyzed and evaluated schools' data to determine the professional development needs of teacher and administrators in the district. Aggregated, analyzed and evaluated district/school data to determine the development of a system wide action plan in implementing curriculum and performance standards. Developed and executed a professional development program designed to support the instructional implementation of the math and reading curriculum. Monitored and assessed the effectiveness of the professional development plan on instructional implementation and students' performance. Consulted and Collaborated with the school leadership teams in utilizing

aggregated data to plan school wide directives and develop goals to meet state benchmarks in students' performance. Planned and facilitated workshops for the district and regional staff. Designed and implemented needs assessment plan to determine the strengths and weakness of the instructional staff and the administration. Coached and mentored staff in effective instructional practices. Collaborated with team members to plan and administer the transitional training for the new curriculum adopted by the New York City Board of Education. Co-labored with colleagues in writing and applying for educational grants. Developed and monitored the monthly expenditure reports and the annual fiscal budgeting for professional development site

Regional Staff Developer, New York Public School 305, 120 Monroe Street, Brooklyn, NY 11216 Supervisor: Charelle Manson (099) 000.3962
Hours: 35-50/per week
8/1999-10/2002
Created and executed a professional development plan based on aggregated data to assist in improving students' performance on state assessments. Developed and implemented workshops in effective instructional practices and strategies. Assisted the leadership team in creating an annual comprehensive education plan based upon aggregated data. Trained staff in analyzing student's data for the purpose of planning differentiated instruction. Assisted in implementing an academic intervention plan which increased the math and reading scores of students and as a direct result the school was removed from the states low performing schools list. Assessed and Evaluated staff's strengths and weaknesses for the purpose of determining professional development needs. Counseled and conferred with teachers to assist in meeting their instructional needs. Developed individualized professional development plans for teachers to assist in improving their instructional practices. Developed and implemented creative curriculum manuals to meet the needs staff members. Developed and implemented workshops for the Balanced Literacy program adopted by the district. Drafted monthly expenditure reports and managed fiscal budgets for professional development. Evaluated student's strengths and weaknesses based on ongoing assessments and developed professional development goals to meet their needs. Supervised the staff and students of the after school academic intervention program. Evaluated the performance of staff based on student achievement and aggregated data. . Recruited, interviewed and hired staff based on school's needs.

TEACHING EXPERIENCE

English Medium Teacher, Ibn Khaldoon Primary Boys School, P.O. Box: 7654, Abu Dhabi, UAE
Supervisor: Mr Smith 971(000) 999.1111
Hours: 30/per week
8/2011-12/2012
Trained, coached and mentored Arabic teachers in effective teaching strategies. Taught, tracked and monitored students' mastery of English as a second language. Planned, prepared and delivered instructional activities that facilitated active learning experiences for English Second Language Students. Identified and selected different instructional resources and methods to meet students' varying needs. Established and communicated clear objectives for all learning activities. Observed and evaluated students' performance and development. Tracked and monitored the progress of individual students. Provided a variety of learning materials and resources for use in educational activities. Managed student behavior in the classroom by establishing and enforcing rules and procedures. Use relevant technology to support instruction.

Fort Bend Independent School District, 16431 Lexington Blvd., Sugar Land, TX 77479: Rorschach Elementary School
Supervisor: Mrs. Julian (000) 230.1000
Hours: 35/per week
8/2008-6/2009
Served as team leader for third grade teachers on the School Leadership Team. Served as the liaison between staff and Administration on educational and pedagogical issues. Aggregated and analyze student data for the purpose of planning and meeting the school's academic benchmarks. Collaborated with the administrative team in assessing the needs of the staff and students for the specific purpose of improving school climate and academic performance. Responsible for implementing and assessing the success of the goals and objective of the annual plan. Planned and administered new directives and programs based on school wide data. Created and provided online instruction and assessments for teachers and students. Trained and implemented the new math program and math initiatives. Monitored students' academic performance and evaluated their academic achievements. Developed and implemented lessons to provide differentiate instruction to meet the various levels of students' academic needs.

Teacher, New York City Board of Education Supervisor:
Steven Harley (000) 123.4567
Hours: 35-50/per week
9/1991-6/1997

Planned weekly and monthly lessons based upon a Thematic and Interdisciplinary approach. Monitored students' academic performance and evaluated their achievement. Analyzed and evaluated student data for the purpose of planning to meet their academic needs. Evaluated and implemented curriculum to meet New York State's academic standards. Planned and administered new directives and programs based on aggregated data collected from students' performance and staff's needs. Facilitated workshops for professional development. Collaborated and assisted the school leadership team in creating an annual school-wide plan to improve the school climate and academic performance of students.

TRAINING/PROFESSIONAL KNOWLEDGE

- Microsoft Applications: PowerPoint, Word, Excel
- Educational Leadership (1999-2000)
- School Based Leadership Team (2000-2001)
- Coaching and Mentoring (2002)
- Data Drive Assessments (2003)
- Balanced Literacy (2003)
- Peer Collaboration (2003)
- Conflict Resolution (2004)
- Public Speaking/Presentation (2001)
- Data Team Training (2008)
- ESL Trainer and Coordinator (2011)

Online Resources for Service Members

The Army's Official Transition Website
Employment FAQ, Leaders FAQ and Transition FAQ
https://www.acap.army.mil/faq.aspx

Go Army's Military Internships
http://www.goarmy.com/benefits/education-benefits/army-education/army-college-programs/internships.html

Department of Labor (DOL) Office of the Assistant Secretary for Veterans' Employment & Training; Staff and Department Directory
http://www.dol.gov/vets/aboutvets/contacts/main.htm

U.S. Department of Veteran Affairs
This government agency provides veterans and dependents with a wide range of services, including benefit information, home loans, life insurance, post-traumatic stress disorder facts and burial assistance.

National Call Center for Homeless Veterans: 1-877-424-3838
Nat. Suicide Prevention Lifeline: 1-800-273-TALK (Press "1")
National Veterans Chat Line: www.SuicidePreventionLifeline.org

U.S. VETS: United States Veterans Initiative
U.S. VETS offers many programs and services to veterans, including transitional and affordable housing, job training, career centers, mental health services and counseling. The organization's Advance Women's Program is designed to help women veterans with military sexual trauma, health issues and psychological barriers. http://www.usvetsinc.org/

Walter Reed Army Medical Center
"Help a veteran get the treatment she needs to start rebuilding her life." Walter Reed provides care to past, present and future soldiers who need care.
http://www.wramc.amedd.army.mil/Pages/default.aspx
The Army Wounded Soldier and Family Hotline: 1-800-984-8523

Grace After Fire
Dedicated to female veterans, Grace After Fire is a place to connect with other women service members and their families. Also, veterans can submit questions to fellow veterans.
http://www.graceafterfire.org/

Wounded Warrior Project
In this organization, injured service members get together to support each other and raise awareness about public aid. Wounded soldiers can get benefits counseling, peer mentoring and more. The Wounded Warrior Project also offers programs and services for veterans' loved ones.
http://www.woundedwarriorproject.org/

Iraq and Afghanistan Veterans of America
This organization is the nation's first—and largest—group dedicated to the veterans of the Iraq and Afghanistan wars and their supporters. IAVA teaches veterans how to play a role in the community, connect with others, organize fundraisers and stay informed on issues that are affecting veterans.
http://iava.org/

American Women Veterans Foundation
Dedicated to preserving and promoting the legacy of servicewomen, veterans and their families, American Women Veterans is a good resource for veterans looking for retreats, conferences and outreach campaigns that empower members and their communities. Female service members are also encouraged to continue helping out in their communities and the nation through philanthropy.
http://americanwomenveterans.org/

Veterans of Foreign Wars
The Veterans of Foreign Wars strives to do good things for veterans, their families and their communities. This organization offers assistance through the National Veterans Service, transitioning back into society, troop support programs, post-military help and programs for veterans' family members. http://www.vfw.org/

Military, Veterans & Patriotic Service Organizations of America (MVPSOA)
This organization certifies high-quality national nonprofits that help veterans and their families. MVPSOA provides information about scholarships for the children of military personnel and information on funding memorials and museums that honor those who have served our country.
http://www.mvpsoa.org/

National Archives: Veterans Information, Aid and Benefits
This website offers a robust list of government services, including resources for a veteran's specific military branch. Plus, veterans can find out about government assistance in their communities. www.archives.gov/veterans/other-resources/benefits-aid.html

Substance Abuse and Mental Health Services Administration
The Substance Abuse and Mental Health Services Administration offers information about suicide prevention, addiction and trauma. Veterans can also learn to cope with fear and anxiety and deal with grief. http://www.samhsa.gov/militaryFamilies/

U.S. Office of Personal Management's Government-Wide Veterans Employment
On November 9, 2009, President Barack Obama signed Executive Order 13518, Employment of Veterans in the Federal Government, which established the Veterans Employment Initiative. This website is the result. It's helpful for veterans who are looking for a job because it helps the government recruit and employ U.S. veterans. http://fedshirevets.gov/Index.aspx

Student Veterans of America
This organization ensures that veterans are successful in the transition from combat to the classroom by helping them develop student veteran groups on college campuses across the United States. Also, veterans can support fellow student veterans here.
http://www.studentveterans.org/

The American Legion
As the nation's largest veteran service organization, the American Legion is committed to mentoring programs in communities across America, advocating for patriotism and honor, promoting strong national security and supporting service members and veterans.
http://www.legion.org/

Employer Support of the Guard and Reserves (ESGR)
A Department of Defense office, established in 1972, to promote cooperation and understanding between Reserve component Service members and their civilian employers and to assist in the resolution of conflicts from an employee's military commitment.
http://www.esgr.mil/

Tag Crowd
Is a web application for visualizing word frequencies in any text by creating what is popularly known as a word cloud, text cloud or tag cloud. You can use Tag word for a variety of useful purposes to digest resumés in a single glance. Can help you when submitting resumés via applicant tracking software.
http://tagcrowd.com/

G.I. Jobs
Is a website that connects you with military friendly recruiters. A guide to post military assistance. It also provide a military to civilian pay calculator to help you get an idea of what you will need to earn to be equivalent to your military pay.
http://calculator.gijobs.com/

For more resources, visit
http://www.archives.gov/veterans/employment-resources.html

Glossary of Military Terms

Army - 50,000 + soldiers. Typically commanded by a lieutenant general or higher, an army combines two or more corps.

Battalion - a large body of 300-1200 that usually consists of two to seven companies; troops ready for battle

Brigade - 3,000 to 5,000 solders. A brigade headquarters commands the tactical operation of two to five attached battalions. Normally commanded by a colonel with a command sergeant major as senior Non Commissioned Officer
Regiment-

Company - is a military unit typically consisting of 80–250 Soldiers usually commanded by a Captain or a Major. Most companies are formed of three to six platoons although the exact number may vary by country, unit type, and structure. Several companies are grouped to form a battalion or brigade, or regiment.

Corps - 20,000 to 45,000 soldiers. Two to five divisions constitute a corps, which is typically commanded by a lieutenant general. As the deployable level of command required to synchronize and sustain combat operations, the corps provides the framework for multi- national operations.

Detachment - a group of troops, aircraft, or ships sent away on a separate mission

Detail - a small detachment of troops/officers given special duty

Division - 10,000 to 15,000 soldiers. Usually consisting of three brigade-sized elements and commanded by a major general, divisions are numbered and assigned missions based on their structures. The division performs major tactical operations for the corps and can conduct sustained battles and engagements.

Group - Two or more Squadrons form a Group. In the Air Force, Groups are usually based upon assignment of squadrons with similar functions. For example, the Supply Squadron, Transportation, and Aircraft Maintenance Squadron would be assigned to the Logistics Group.

Platoon - 16 to 44 soldiers. A platoon is led by a lieutenant with an Non-Commissioned Officer as second in command, and consists of two to four squads or sections.

Section: Two or more airmen can form a "section." Generally, the section is the place (duty section) where the person works.

Soldier - single US Army member

Squad - 9 to 10 soldiers. Typically commanded by a sergeant or staff sergeant, a squad or section is the smallest element in the Army structure, and its size is dependent on its function.

Task Force - an armed force organized for a special operation.

Airforce

Airman - single Air Force member

Flight - Two or more airmen can form a flight. Two or more sections can also form a flight. It depends upon how the Squadron is organized

Squadron - an operational unit in an air force consisting of two or more flights of aircraft and the personnel required to fly them form a squadron. The squadron is the lowest level of command with a headquarters element (example, a Squadron Commander, or Squadron First Sergeant).

Wing - Two or more groups compose a Wing. There is only one Wing on an Air Force base, and the Wing Commander is quite often considered to be the "Installation Commander." There are two types of Wings: Composite and Objective

Navy

Navy - A nation's entire military organization for sea warfare and defense, including vessels, personnel, and shore establishments.

Fleet - (naval) A fleet, or naval fleet, is a large formation of warships, and the largest formation in any navy. A fleet at sea is the direct equivalent of an army on land.

NOTE: THE US Army Organization structure can be found in DA Pamphlet 10-1 at http://usmilitary.about.com/cs/airforce/a/aforganization.htm

About Chief Raymond

Chief Warrant Officer Dylan Raymond is a graduate of the University of Maryland University College and holds a Bachelors degree in Business Administration. He is a certified Professional in Human Resources Management (PHR) with more than fifteen years of recruiting experience.

Chief rose through the ranks from private/E-1 through Master Sergeant and was later appointed to Warrant Officer. He served as a Drill Sergeant and for 4 ½ years as top producing Field Army Recruiter. He served in various other roles in the military from entry-level through advising senior officers at the executive level. He reviewed thousands of resumés and provides coaching and mentoring to military service members, family members and civilians alike.

Chief Raymond has two deployments: one to Iraq and the other to Kuwait. He is the recipient of several awards: the US Army Recruiters Gold Badge, the Recruiter Ring for Recruiting Excellence, the Texas ESGR Volunteer of the Year award, Reserve Officer Association Warrant Officer of the Year award, CW4 Michael J Novosel Outstanding Warrant Officer of the Year Award and the General Douglas MacArthur Leadership Award.

Chief Raymond is married and the father of 4 girls.

www.ingramcontent.com/pod-product-compliance
Lightning Source LLC
Chambersburg PA
CBHW051703170526
45167CB00002B/511